NATIONAL TESTS practice papers

FOR THE YEAR 2004

Maths, English and Science

Book 2 Levels 4–7

AGE 13–14
Key Stage 3

practice papers

Contents	Page
Introduction and notes to parents	
The National Tests: A Summary	iii
Maths	
Maths at Key Stage 3	1
Paper 1 (non-calculator paper)	2
Paper 2 (calculator paper)	19
Mental Maths Test	34
Answers	39
National Curriculum Levels	47
English	
English at Key Stage 3	48
Reading Paper	52
Writing Paper	57
Shakespeare	58
Henry V	59
Twelfth Night	63
Macbeth	66
Answers	71
National Curriculum Levels	78
Science	
Science at Key Stage 3	79
Science Test	81
Answers	105
National Curriculum Levels	108

Acknowledgements
The authors and publisher would like to thank the copyright owners of the following for permission to reproduce material in this book.

Portrait of the Artist as a Young Dog, Dylan Thomas, J.M. Dent and Sons Ltd and the Trustees for the copyright of the late Dylan Thomas.

'Warning' by Jenny Joseph, from *A Rose in the Afternoon*, J.M. Dent and Sons Ltd.

Every effort has been made to trace and acknowledge ownership of copyright material but if any have been inadvertently overlooked, the publisher will be pleased to make the necessary alterations at the first opportunity.

First published 2003
exclusively for WHSmith by
Hodder & Stoughton Educational,
a division of Hodder Headline Ltd
338 Euston Road
London NW1 3BH

Text and illustrations © Hodder & Stoughton Educational 2003

All rights reserved. No part of this publication may be reproduced or transmitted in any form or by any means, electronic or mechanical, including photocopying, recording or any information storage and retrieval system, without permission in writing from the publisher.

A CIP record for this book is available from the British Library.

Authors: Steve Mills and Hilary Koll (Maths), Christine Moorcroft and Ray Barker (English), Terry Hudson (Science)

ISBN 0340 81390 3

Impression   5 4 3 2 1
Year   2004 2003

Printed and bound by Hobbs The Printers, Totton, Hampshire

NOTE: The tests, questions and advice in this book are not reproductions of the official test materials sent to schools. The official testing process is supported by guidance and training for teachers in setting and marking tests and interpreting the results. The results achieved in the tests in this book may not be the same as those achieved in the official tests.

Introduction

The National Tests: A Summary
What are the National Tests?

Children who attend state schools in England and Wales sit National Tests (commonly known as SATs) at the ages of 7, 11 and 14, usually at the beginning of May. They may also sit optional tests in the intervening years – many schools have chosen to adopt these tests. The test results are accompanied by an assessment by the child's teacher (at Key Stage 3 this also covers non-tested subjects such as History or Geography).

The results are used by the school to assess each child's level of knowledge and progress in English and Maths at Key Stage 1, and in English, Maths and Science at Key Stages 2 and 3. They also provide useful guidance for the child's next teacher when he or she is planning the year's work.

The educational calendar for children aged 5–14 is structured as follows:

Key Stage	Year	Age by end of year	National Test
1 (KS1)	1	6	
	2	7	KEY STAGE 1
	3	8	Optional Year 3
2 (KS2)	4	9	Optional Year 4
	5	10	Optional Year 5
	6	11	KEY STAGE 2
3 (KS3)	7	12	Optional Year 7
	8	13	Optional Year 8
	9	14	KEY STAGE 3

Timetable

Key Stage 3 pupils will sit their tests on **4–7 May 2004**, with the following timetable (but check with the school as dates may change):

Tuesday 4 May	Wednesday 5 May	Thursday 6 May	Friday 7 May
AM SESSION (UP TO 12 NOON)			
Science Paper 1 *1 hour*	**Mental Mathematics Test A and Test C** *20 minutes* **Mathematics Paper 1** *1 hour*	**English Reading Paper** *1 hour (plus 15 minutes reading time)* **Mental Mathematics Test B** *20 minutes*	**English Shakespeare Paper** *1 hour 15 minutes*
PM SESSION (AFTER 12 NOON)			
Science Paper 2 *1 hour*	**Mathematics Paper 2** *1 hour*	**English Writing Paper** *45 minutes (including 15 minutes planning)*	

Introduction

Levels

National targets have been set for students' results in the National Tests, as follows:

LEVEL	AGE 7 (Key Stage 1)	AGE 11 (Key Stage 2)	AGE 14 (Key Stage 3)
8			
7			
6			
5			
4			
3			
2			
2a			
2b			
2c			
1			

- BELOW EXPECTED LEVEL
- EXPECTED LEVEL
- ABOVE EXPECTED LEVEL
- EXCEPTIONAL

Results

Your child's school will send you a report indicating his or her levels in the tests and the teacher assessment.

The school's overall test results will be included in local and national league tables, which are published in most newspapers.

What can parents do to help?

While it is never a good idea to encourage cramming, you can help your child to succeed by:

- Making sure he or she has enough food, sleep and leisure time during the test period.
- Encouraging your child to practise important skills such as writing and reading, spelling and mental arithmetic.
- Telling him or her what to expect in the test, such as important symbols and key words.
- Helping him or her to be comfortable in test conditions including working within a time limit, reading questions carefully and understanding different ways of answering.

Maths

Maths at Key Stage 3

Guidance for parents

The Key Stage 3 National Test in Maths consists of two written papers, one to be taken without a calculator and the other with a calculator, and a mental maths test. The tests will cover aspects of Number and Algebra, Shape, Space and Measures and Handling Data.

Levels and tiers of entry

Your child will be entered for one of four tiers. Your child's teacher will make a judgement about which of the tiers to enter your child for.

This book includes two written papers that cover the most popular tiers of entry. Paper 1 covers levels 4–6 and Paper 2 covers levels 5–7. The mental maths test includes questions at levels 4–7. To gain an idea of the level at which your child is working, use the table on page 47.

Setting the Maths Tests

Equipment needed

Paper 1: pen, pencil, ruler, rubber.

Paper 2: pen, pencil, ruler, rubber, protractor or angle measurer, pair of compasses, scientific or graphic calculator, tracing paper and a mirror (optional).

Mental Maths Test: pencil and rubber.

A clock or watch with a second hand is useful for ensuring times for each question on the mental test are appropriate.

The written papers

A formula sheet is included for each test. Encourage your child to refer to it where necessary. Each written paper lasts for **1 hour**, starting with easier questions and gradually becoming more difficult.

The mental maths test

The mental test should take approximately **20 minutes** to give. Cut out pages 35 and 36 so you can read them aloud to your child. Your child should use the sheets on pages 34, 37 and 38 for his or her answers.

Marking the tests

Next to each question in the written tests is a number indicating how many marks the question or part of the question is worth. Enter your child's mark into the circle above, using the answer pages (39–46) to help you decide how many points to award.

The answer pages also offer advice, provide information about common errors made by pupils and include tips to help your child understand the mathematical ideas.

Find your child's total score from the written papers and refer to page 47 for information about the level at which your child might be working.

Maths Test
Paper 1

You *cannot* use a calculator for any questions in Paper 1.

Formulae

You might need to use these formulae.

AREA

Circle

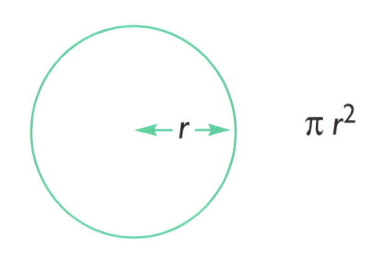

πr^2

Take π as 3.14.

Triangle

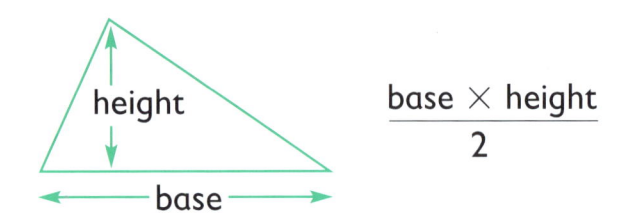

$$\frac{base \times height}{2}$$

Parallelogram

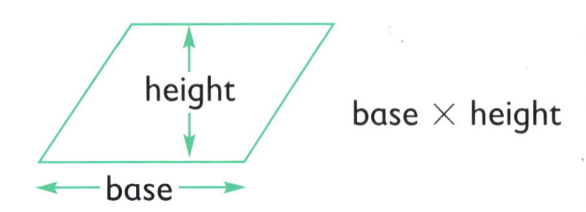

base × height

Trapezium

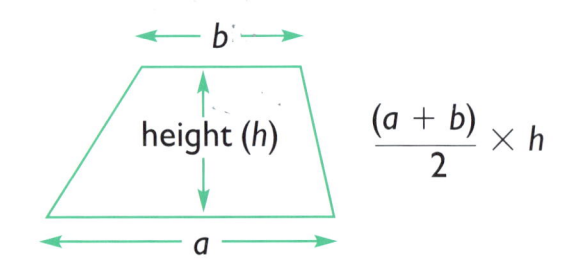

$$\frac{(a + b)}{2} \times h$$

LENGTH

Circle

circumference = $2\pi r$

VOLUME

Prism

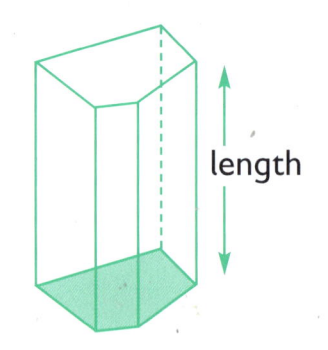

area of cross-section × length

You will need: pen, pencil, rubber, ruler.

Practice Questions

Write one number in each box to make each equation correct.

Example

144 + 30 = ☐ **174**

a ✏ 168 + 40 = ☐ 208

b ✏ 835 − 40 = ☐ 795

c ✏ 100 − ☐ 28 = 72

d ✏ 10 × ☐ 42 = 420

Maths Test
Paper 1

1 Write one number in each box to make each equation correct.

a   34 × [1000] = 3400

b   900 ÷ [6] = 150

c   [128] − 50 = 78

d   [60] × 6 = 360

e   [121] ÷ [11] = 11

TOTAL 5

2 A square has **4 lines of reflective symmetry**:

and has **rotational symmetry of order 4**:

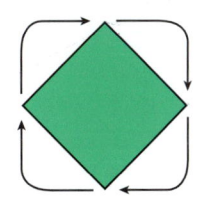

Here are some shapes.

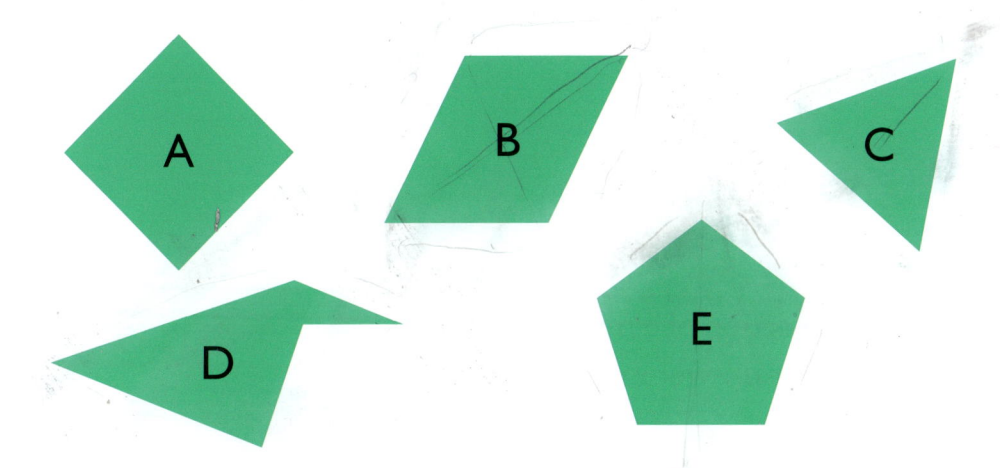

A B C D E

Fill in the missing numbers in the table below.

	lines of reflective symmetry	rotational symmetry of order
Shape A	**4**	**4**
Shape B	2	4
Shape C	1	3
Shape D	0	4
Shape E	1	5

Maths Test – Paper 1

Shape symmetry

4

TOTAL

4

Maths Test – Paper 1

Fractions

3 In a shop, some lengths of cane are being measured with a metre stick. Here are three canes labelled A, B and C.

1 metre

A

B

C

a What fraction of a metre is Cane A?

$\dfrac{3}{10}$

1

b What fraction of a metre is Cane B? Give your answer in its simplest form.

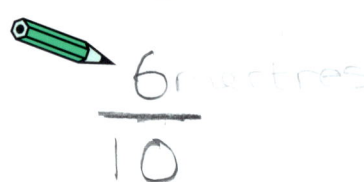

$\dfrac{6}{10}$

1

c What percentage of a metre is Cane C?

80%

1

TOTAL 3

6

Maths Test – Paper 1

d Another cane, Cane D, is exactly $\frac{2}{5}$ of a metre.

Give the length of Cane D in centimetres.

Cane D = _____40_____ cm

(working shown: 100, 100 ÷ 5 = 20, 20 × 2 = 40)

1

e Mr Kumar buys 10 pieces of **Cane A**.
If these canes were placed end-to-end in a straight line, how long would the line be?

20 metres

1

f Another cane, Cane E, is $\frac{2}{3}$ of a metre.

One of the statements below is true. Tick the true statement.

Cane E is shorter than Cane B.	✓
Cane E is longer than Cane C.	
Cane E is longer than Cane B but shorter than Cane C.	
Cane E is shorter than Cane B but longer than Cane A.	

1

TOTAL 3

Maths Test – Paper 1

Money

4a A teacher collects money from pupils for a school residential trip.
Each pupil pays **12** instalments of **£10.25**.
What is the total amount of money each pupil pays for the trip?

£ 10.25
× 12
2050
12025

£123
275

b Each pupil takes exactly **£20** spending money on the school trip.
There are **30** pupils.
How much spending money do the pupils take in total?

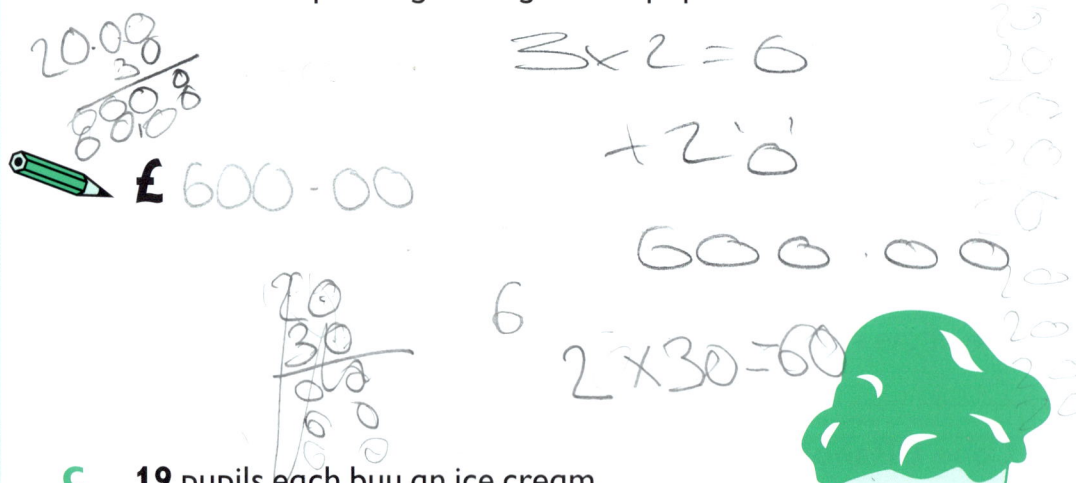

£ 600.00

3×2 = 6
+20
600.00
2×30=60

c 19 pupils each buy an ice cream.
The ice creams cost **50p**.
How much money do they spend on ice creams in total?

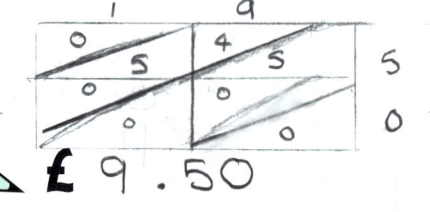

£ 9.50

TOTAL 3

Maths Test – Paper 1

d Leroy spends **£8.48** on a T-shirt.
He pays with a **£20** note.
How much change does he get?

✏️ £11.52

1

e Claire writes down how much she spent while on the trip.

Ice creams	£1.50
T-shirt	£8.48
Cap	£4.99
Sweets	83p

How much did she spend in total?

✏️ £15.90

1

TOTAL
2

Maths Test – Paper 1

Probability

5 A bag of money contains different coins.

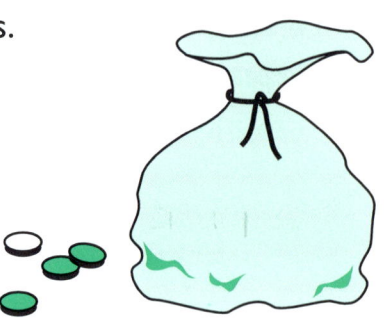

It has **six 20p** coins, **three 10p** coins, **two 5p** coins and a **1p coin**.

a What is the **probability** that one coin picked from the bag at random is a **1p**? Write your answer as a **fraction**.

$\frac{1}{12}$

b Draw a cross on this line to show the probability that the coin is a 20p.

impossible   certain

0 ———|———|———|———X———|———|———| 1

c Draw a cross on this line to show the probability that the coin is not a 5p.

impossible   certain

0 ———|———|———|———|———X———|———| 1

d Draw a cross on this line to show the probability that the coin is a silver coin.

impossible ———————————————— certain
0   1
                                          X

Davina decides to pick a coin, record it and **put the coin back**. She does this **60 times**. She organises her results into a table.

Coin	Frequency
20p	29
10p	12
5p	13
1p	6

e Davina looks at her results and says:

"There is a greater probability of picking a 5p coin than a 10p."

Explain why Davina is **wrong**.

There's 3 10p coins and only 2 5p coins so you have a bigger posibility of getting a 10.

Maths Test – Paper 1

Using letters

6 Sam has some tropical fish in a tank.

Call the number of fish he has **n**.

a Sam puts 4 more fish into the tank.

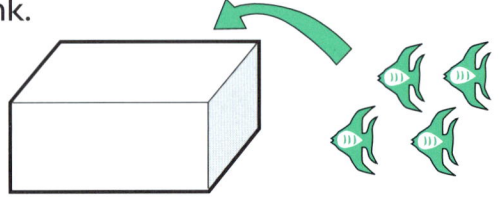

Write an expression to show how many fish are now in the tank.

✏️ _n 4_

b Sam takes the new fish out so that he starts again with **n** fish in his tank.

He takes out exactly **one-half** of the fish in the tank and puts them into a bowl.

Write an expression to show how many fish are now in the tank.

✏️ _2n_

1

1

TOTAL

2

12

Sam starts again with **n** fish in the tank.

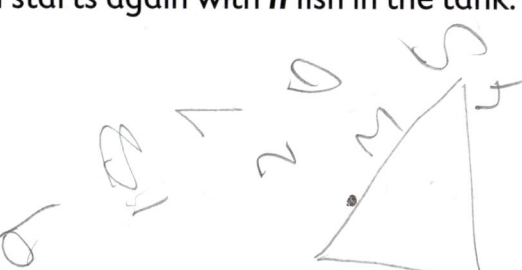

c Write an expression to show how many fish Sam would have if he had **double** this number of fish.

2n

d Sam's dad has exactly **20 times** as many fish as Sam has. Write an expression to show how many fish Sam's dad has.

20n

e These expressions show how many fish are in these two tanks.

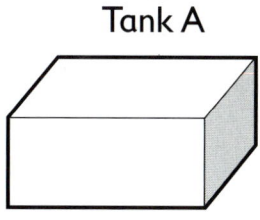

Tank A

$3n - 3$

Tank B

$3(n - 3)$

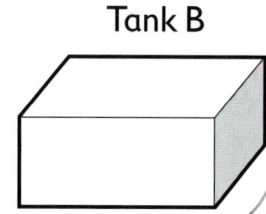

Do the tanks hold the same number?
Explain your answer.

when the brackets are Removed angle

Maths Test – Paper 1

Sequences

7 Here is a sequence of shapes made from white and coloured triangles.

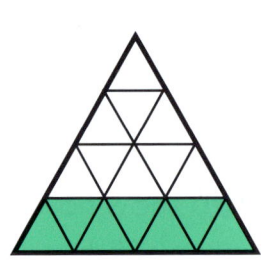

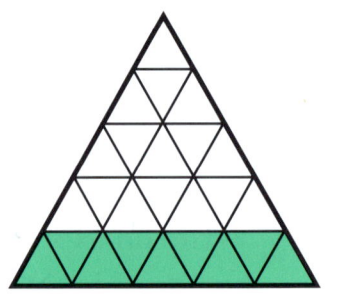

Shape 1   Shape 2   Shape 3   Shape 4

a Complete the table by filling in the missing numbers for Shape **7** and Shape **10**.

Shape number	1	2	3	4	7	10
Number of coloured triangles	3	5	7	9	11	13
Number of white triangles	1	4	9	16	25	36

1   2×2   3×3   4×4   5×5   6×6

b Complete the table by writing **expressions** for Shape **n**.

Shape number	1	2	3	4	n
Number of coloured triangles	3	5	7	9	
Number of white triangles	1	4	9	16	

TOTAL 4

Maths Test – Paper 1

c Write an expression to show the **total** number of triangles used to make Shape **n**.

[handwritten working: 2n+3, 2n+3, 2n, 4n]

d For a different sequence of shapes, the number of **squares** used can be expressed as **2n + 3**.

[handwritten table:
n	1	2	3	4
s	5	7	9	11

+2 +2 +2]

Which of the sets of shapes below shows Shapes 1 and 2 in this sequence?

Set 1

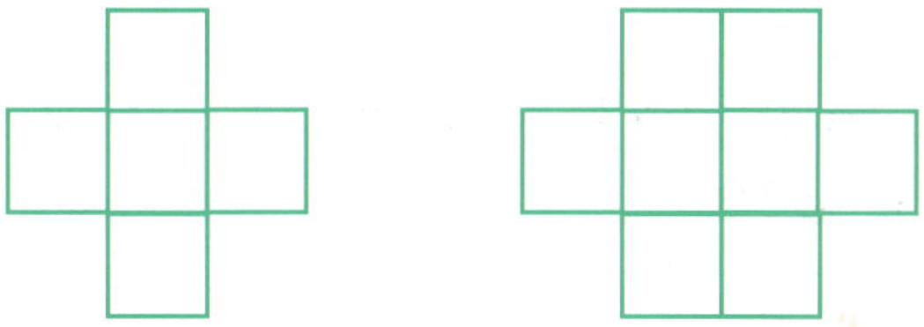

Shape 1   Shape 2

Set 2

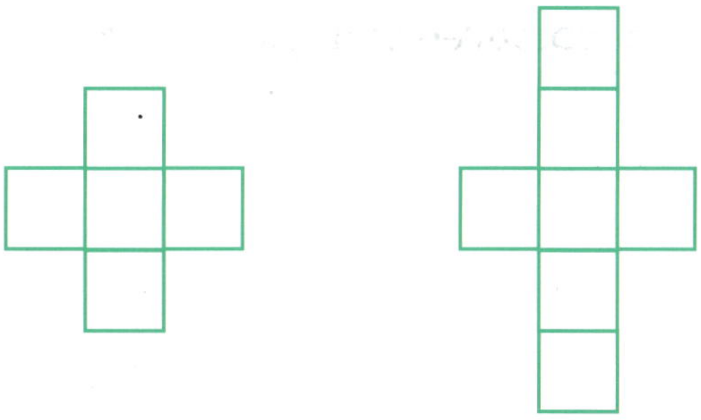

Shape 1   Shape 2 ✓

Set 3

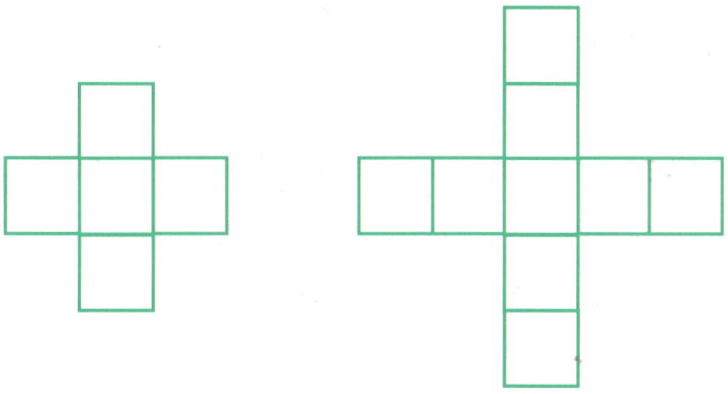

Shape 1   Shape 2

Set _____

1

TOTAL

2

15

Angles

8 This shape is part of a design.

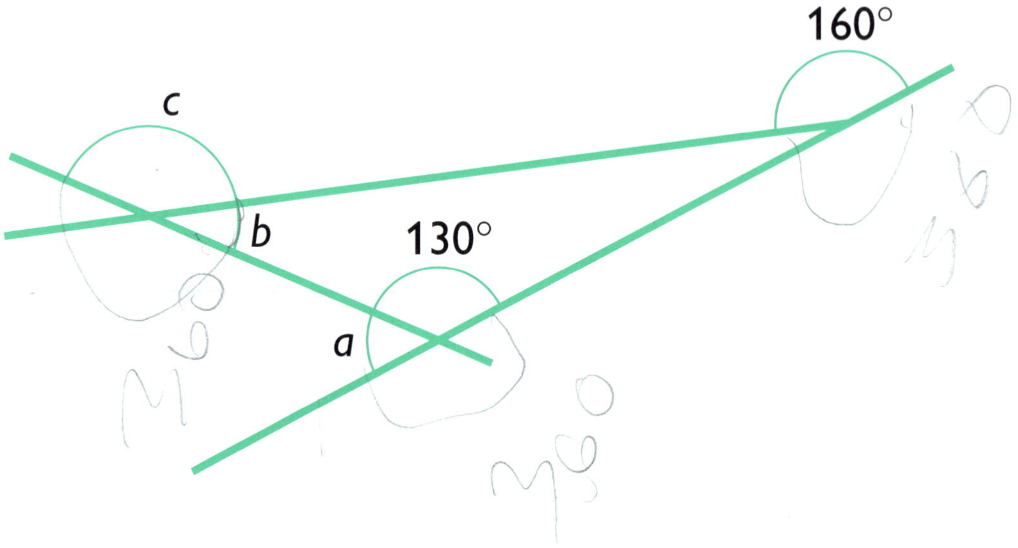

Calculate angles *a*, *b* and *c*.

$a =$ 50° °

$b =$ ______ °

$c =$ ______ °

3

TOTAL

3

9 Aswin has been plotting some lines on a graph.
The line AB is **parallel** to the line CD.

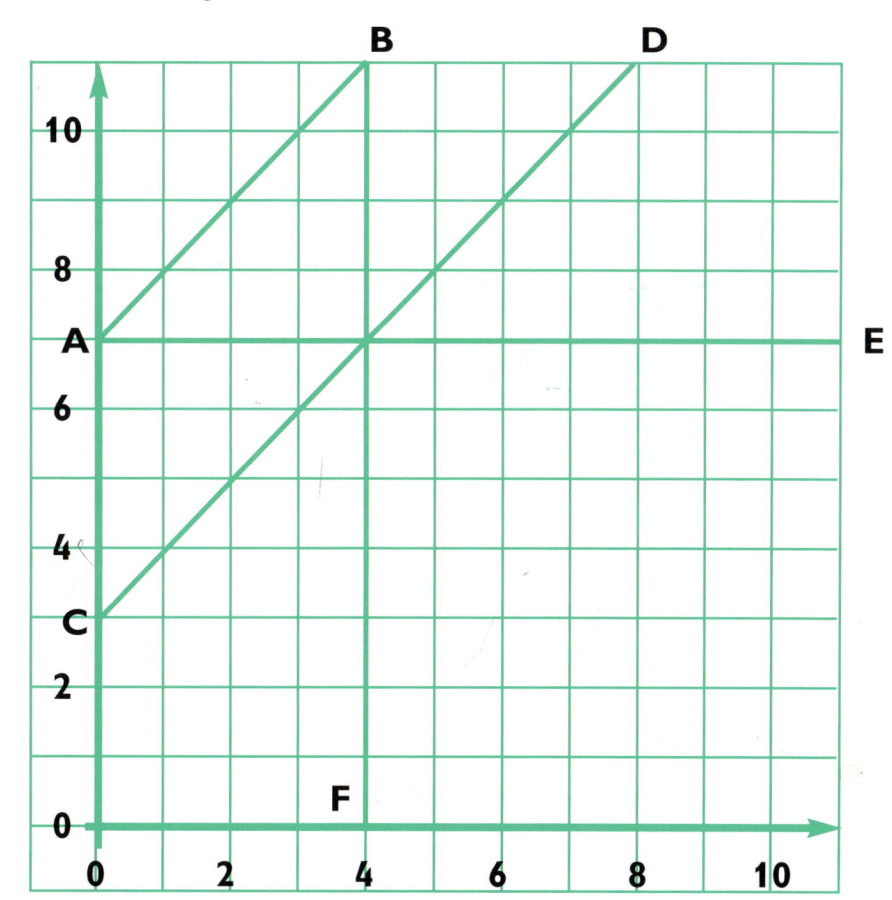

a The equation of the line BF is *x = 4*.
What is the equation of the line AE?

b The line AB has the equation *y = x + 7*.
What is the equation of the line CD?

c On the graph, draw and label the line GH with the equation *y = – x + 10*.

Maths Test – Paper 1

Areas

10 Here are two shapes. They are not drawn to scale.
The area of the trapezium is **three times** the area of the parallelogram.

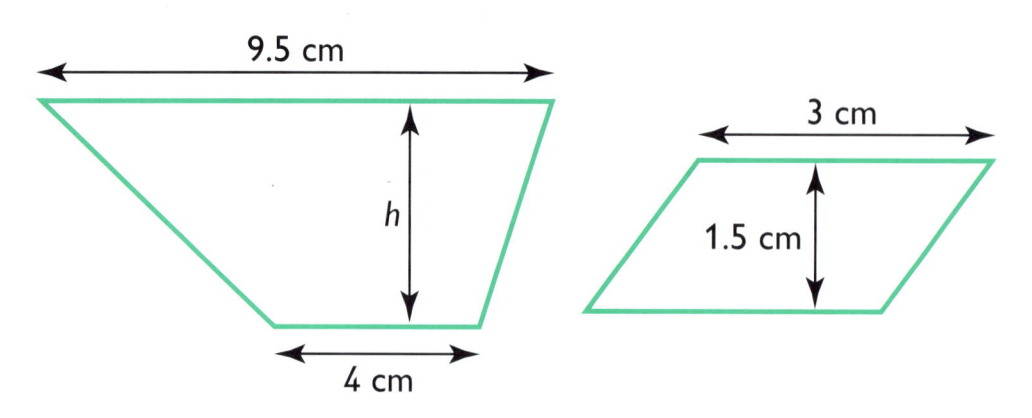

- Trapezium: top = 9.5 cm, bottom = 4 cm, height = h
- Parallelogram: base = 3 cm, height = 1.5 cm

a Calculate the height of the trapezium (h).
Show your working.

Student working:
1.5 × 9.5
× 4
———
9.9
/2

= 4.95

h = ...4.95...... cm

b What is the area of the trapezium below?
Give your answer in terms of y, in its simplest form.

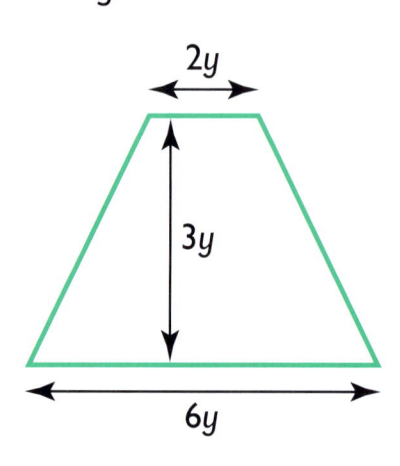

- Trapezium: top = 2y, height = 3y, bottom = 6y

Student working:
6 + 2 = 8/2
× 3 = 12

Area = ____12y____

Maths Test
Paper 2

Formulae

You *can* use a calculator for any questions in Paper 2.

You might need to use these formulae.

AREA

Circle

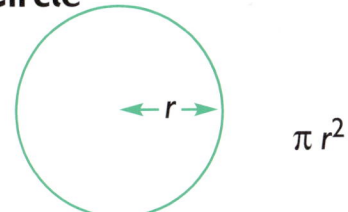

πr^2

Take π as 3.14 or use the π button on your calculator.

Triangle

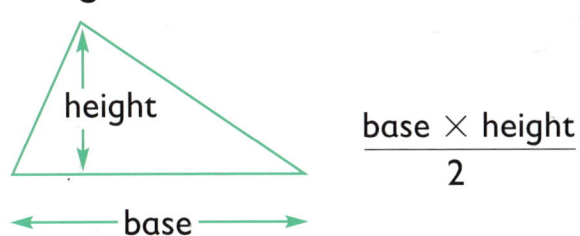

$\dfrac{\text{base} \times \text{height}}{2}$

Parallelogram

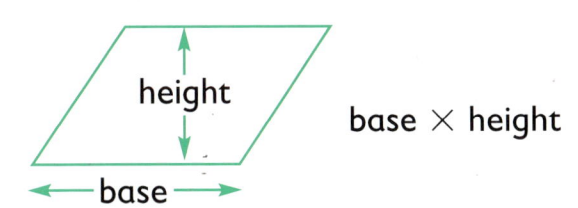

base × height

Trapezium

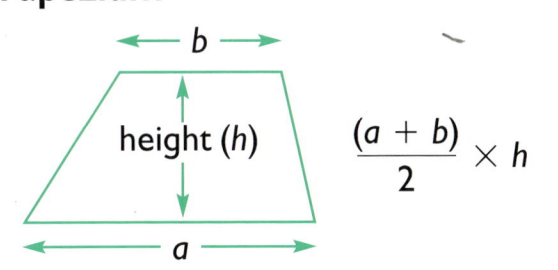

$\dfrac{(a + b)}{2} \times h$

LENGTH

Circle

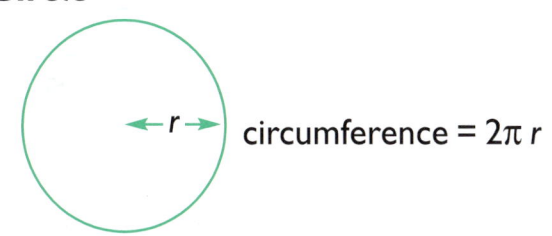

circumference = $2\pi r$

Right-angled triangle

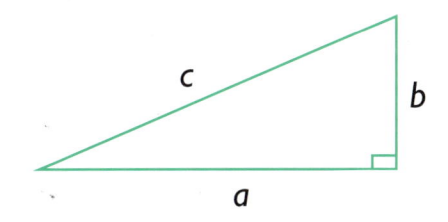

$a^2 + b^2 = c^2$ (Pythagoras' Theorem)

VOLUME

Prism

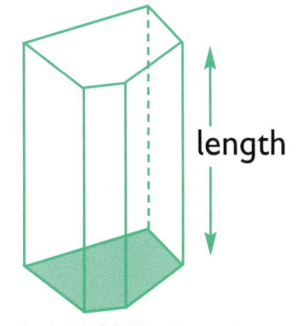

area of cross-section × length

You will need: pen, pencil, rubber, ruler, scientific or graphic calculator, a pair of compasses, protractor, tracing paper, mirror (optional).

Maths Test – Paper 2

Running rates

1 This graph shows the progress of two runners during a 60 metre race.

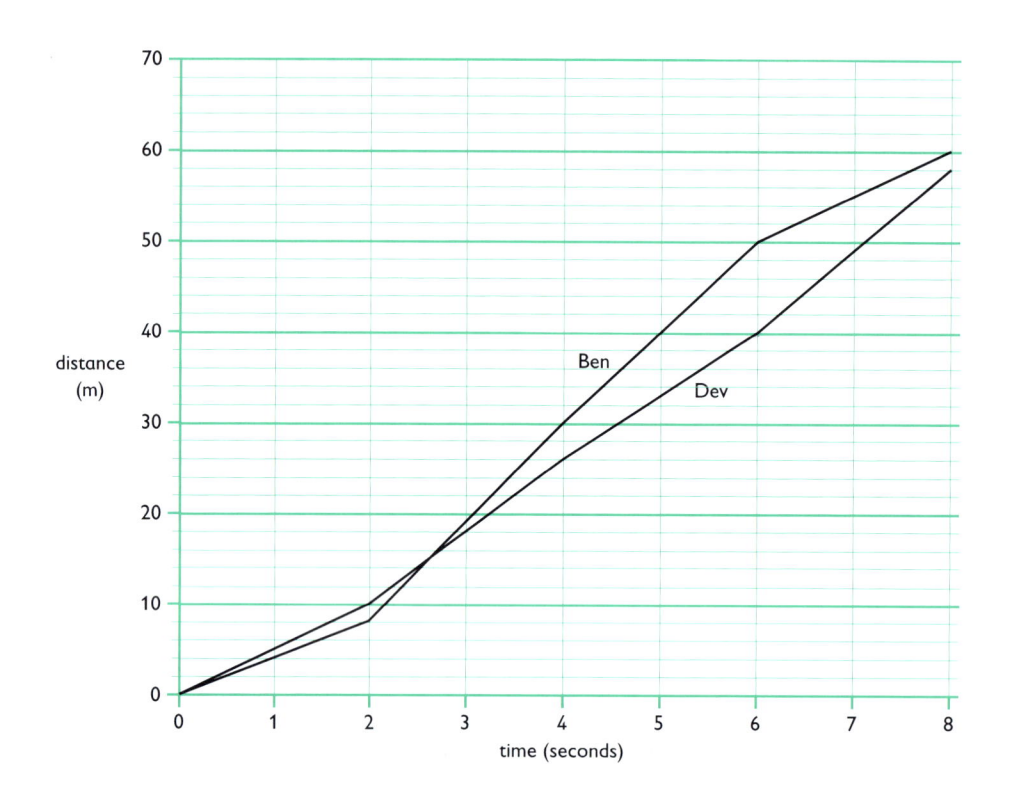

a This table shows the progress of **Dev** during the race. Complete the table, using the graph above.

time interval (s)	distance at start (m)	distance at end (m)	running rate (m)
0–2	0	10	10
2–4	10	26	16
4–6			
6–8			

TOTAL 2

20

Maths Test – Paper 2

This table shows the progress of **Ben** during the race.

time interval (s)	distance at start (m)	distance at end (m)	running rate (m)
0–2	0	8	8
2–4	8	30	22
4–6	30	50	20
6–8	50	60	10

b Use the two tables to help you describe the differences in progress between the two runners during the race.

_____

_____

_____

_____

c Use the graph to see which of the runners won the 60 m race.

21

Maths Test – Paper 2

Square sequences

2 Here is a sequence of shapes made from white and coloured squares.

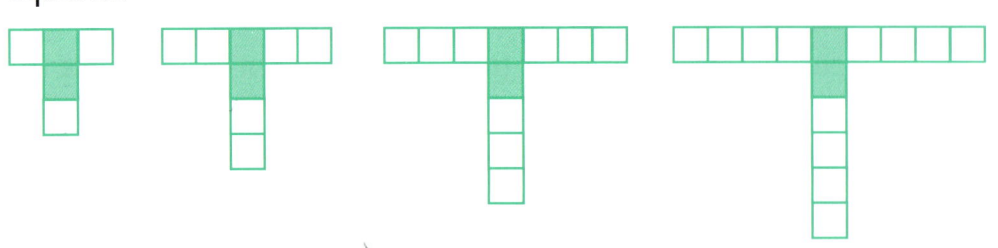

Shape 1   Shape 2   Shape 3   Shape 4

> The rule for finding the **number of squares** in **Shape n** is
>
> 3n + 2

a Venus says:

"You can see that the pattern is 3n + 2 by studying the shapes."

Explain in your own words what you think Venus means.

_____

_____

_____

b How many **white** squares and how many **coloured** squares are in Shape 12?

_36_ white and _24_ coloured squares

22

Maths Test – Paper 2

c A shape in this sequence is made from **62** squares. What is the number of this shape?

Shape __41__

Handwritten working:
62 ÷ 3
= 20.6
= 41.2
Round it down to 41

1

d Here is a new sequence of shapes made from white and coloured squares.

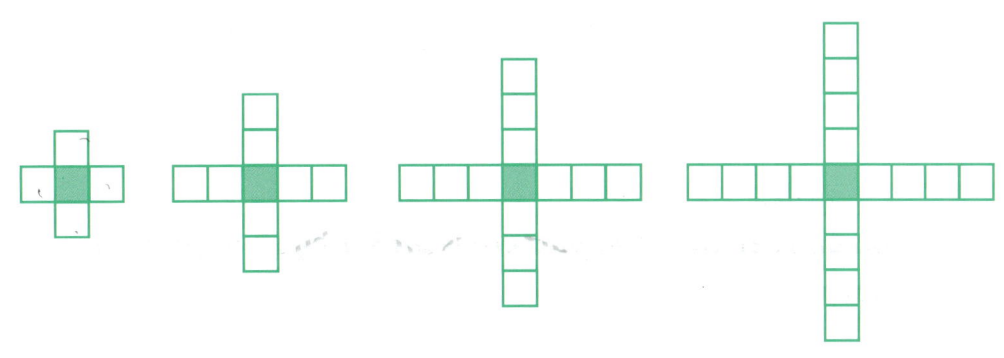

Shape 1   Shape 2   Shape 3   Shape 4

Write a rule for finding the number of squares in **Shape n**.

Handwritten: GOES UP IN 4'S BUT U ADD 1 COLOURED SQURE

Number of squares = __4N+1__

1

TOTAL

2

23

Maths Test – Paper 2

Cubes

3 Here are two shapes made from small cubes. Three of the cubes are coloured.

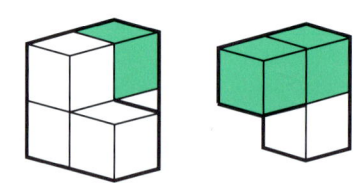

The two shapes are joined together to make a **cuboid**.

a Draw a picture of this **cuboid** on the grid below.
Shade the three coloured cubes on your picture.

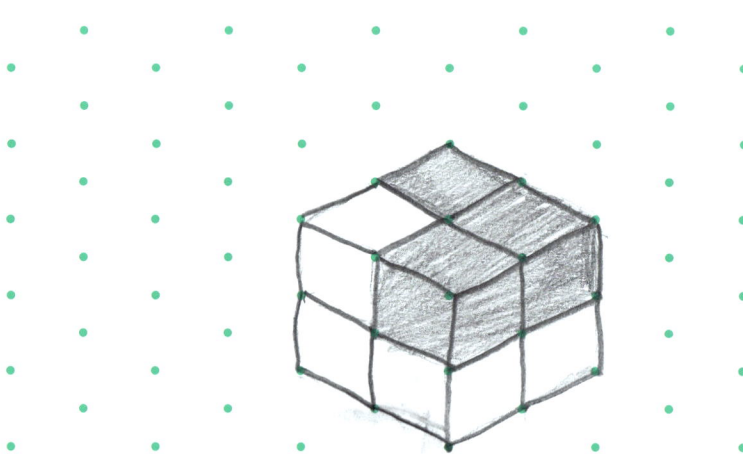

b Each small cube is one centimetre cubed (1 cm³).
Write the dimensions of the cuboid you have drawn.

Length = ...2.... cm   Width = ...2.... cm   Height = ...2.... cm

Here is a drawing of a different cuboid made from centimetre cubes.

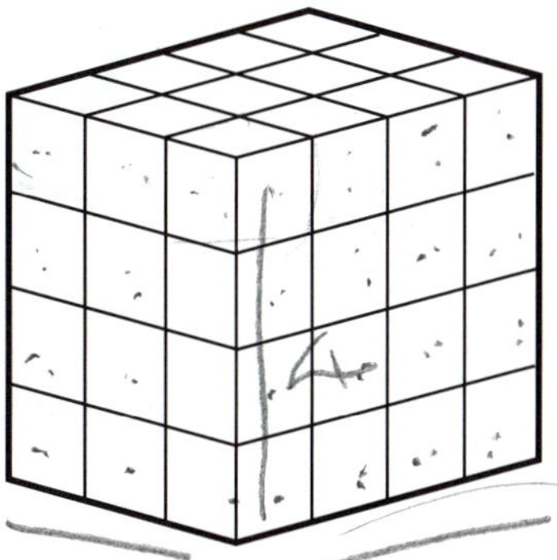

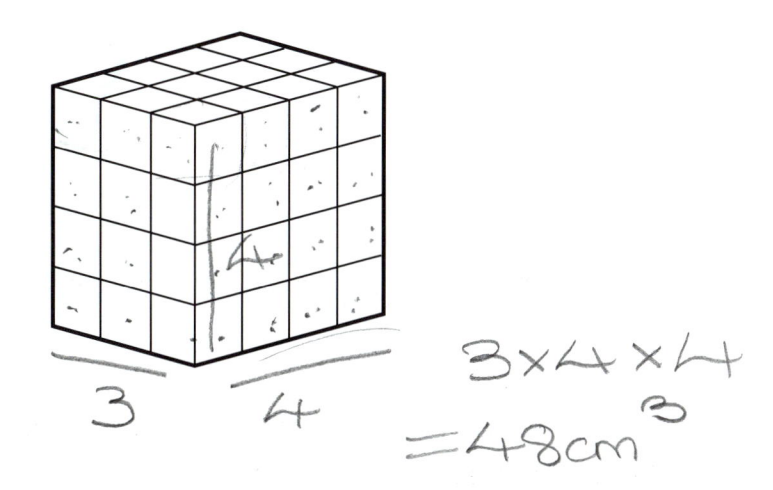

3 4

$3 \times 4 \times 4$

$= 48 cm^3$

c What is the **volume** of this cuboid?

Volume = ...48... cm^3

2

d Jo picks up this cuboid. She looks at it from all angles. She realises that some of the small cubes inside the cuboid cannot be seen from any angle.

How many of the small cubes **cannot** be seen?

24

1

e What fraction of the total number of cubes **can** be seen?

$\frac{24}{100}$ $\frac{12}{50}$ $\frac{6}{25}$

1

TOTAL

4

Maths Test – Paper 2

Equations

4. Jeremy knows that the volume of a cuboid is **268.32 cm³**.
He knows that the height is 12 cm, and that the length is **6 cm greater** than the width.

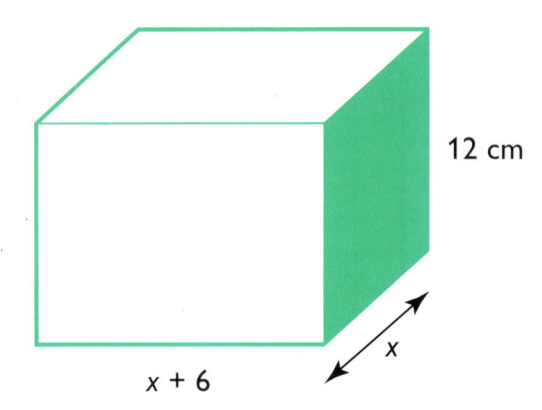

12 cm

x + 6

x

Jeremy writes this equation to show the volume of the cuboid.

$$x(x + 6) \times 12 = 268.32$$

Find the value of x.

You may find this table helpful.

x	x + 6	x (x + 6)	x (x + 6) × 12	
4	10	40	480	too large

x = ...cm

5 When baking cakes, Rob follows this instruction:

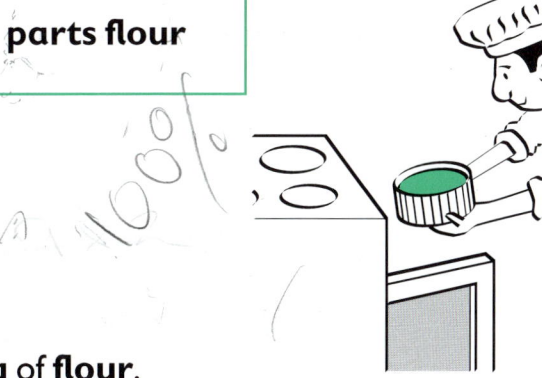

| 2 parts butter   to   7 parts flour |

a In one cake, Rob uses **350 g** of **flour**.
How much butter does he use?

butter = _____ g

b In a second cake, Rob uses **80 g** of **butter**.
How much flour does he use?

flour = _____ g

c Rob makes a third cake. He mixes a total of **1800 g** of **flour and butter**.
How much **flour and butter** does he use?
Show your working.

flour = _____ g   butter = _____ g

Maths Test – Paper 2

Scalene triangle

6 This sketch shows the measurements of a scalene triangle. Angle *a* is not given. The sketch is not to scale.

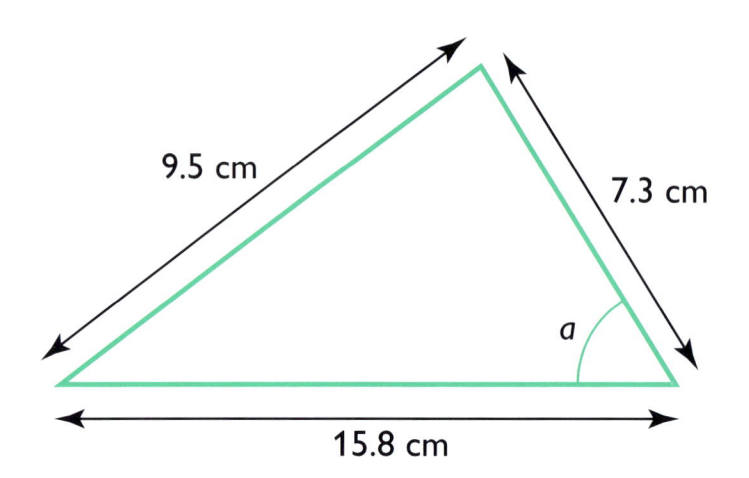

9.5 cm

7.3 cm

a

15.8 cm

a Make an **accurate** full-size drawing of the triangle. You may use a ruler and a pair of compasses.

b Use a protractor to measure angle *a* in your drawing, to the nearest degree.

a = ... °

TOTAL

3

28

7a The **diameter** of a circle is **16 cm**.

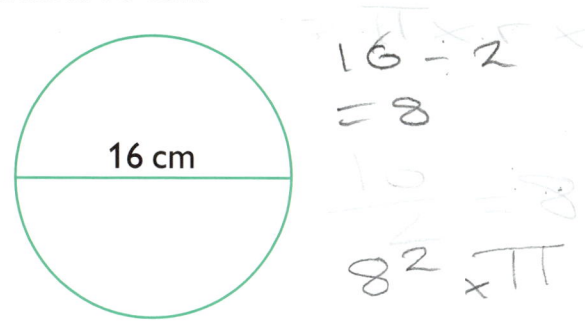

16 cm

Find the **area** of this circle. Take π to be 3.14.
Show your working.

16 ÷ 2 = 8

8² × π

= 201.0619298

Area of circle = 201.06 cm²

b The **circumference** of a different circle is **69 cm** to the nearest centimetre.
Find the **radius** of this circle.
Give your answer to the nearest centimetre.
Show your working.

Radius of circle = ... cm

Maths Test – Paper 2

Sports results

8 During Sports Day some students took part in the cricket ball throwing competition. Their results are shown below.

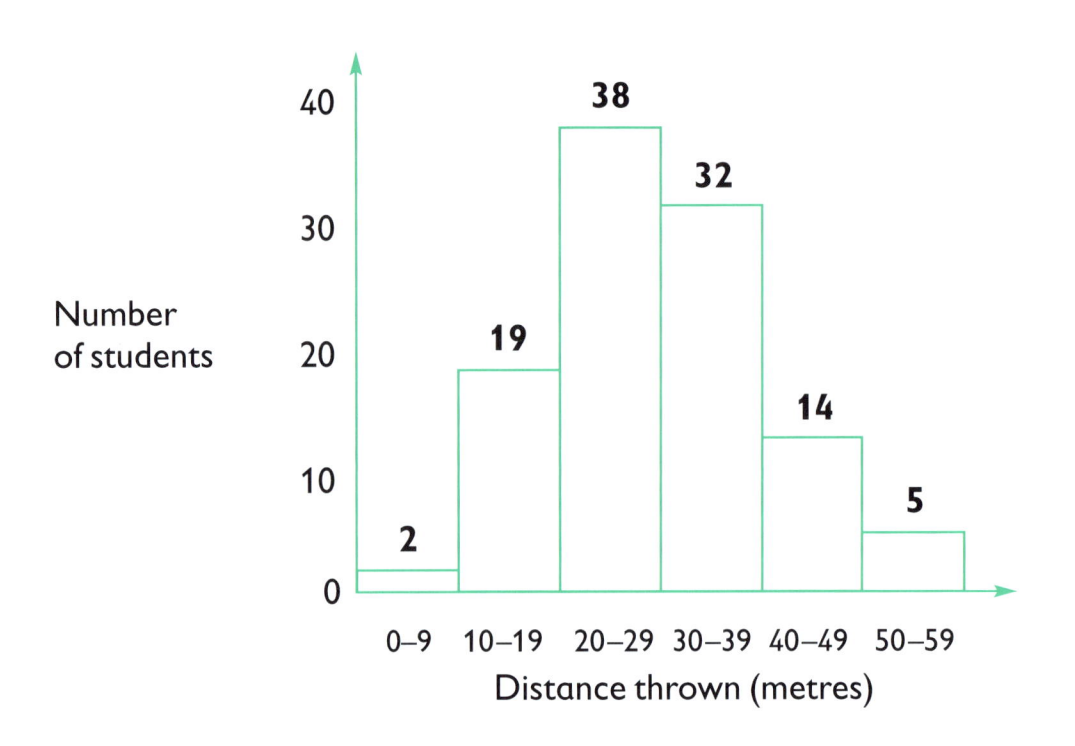

Number of students

Distance thrown (metres)	0–9	10–19	20–29	30–39	40–49	50–59
Number of students	2	19	38	32	14	5

a How many students took part in the competition?

_____

b Serena says:

"Less than half of the students threw further than 25 metres."

Do you think Serena's comment is true or false, or do you think more information is needed? Explain your answer.

_____

_____

_____

c Tanya says:
"*The range of the throws is 59 m.*"

Do you think Tanya's comment is true or false, or do you think more information is needed? Explain your answer.

_____

_____

_____

d Calculate an estimate of the **mean** distance thrown.
Give your answer to 1 decimal place.
You may find this table helpful.

metres	midpoint of bar (x)	number of students (f)	fx
0–9	4.5	2	9
10–19	14.5	19	
20–29	24.5	38	
30–39	34.5	32	
40–49	44.5	14	
50–59	54.5	5	

.... m

TOTAL

31

Maths Test – Paper 2

Simultaneous equations

9 Lucy and Emily have different amounts of money in whole pounds. Call the number of pounds Lucy has p and the number of pounds Emily has q.

If you multiply Lucy's amount by four and then add two, you get three times Emily's amount.
If you multiply Lucy's amount by eight and then subtract two, you get five times Emily's amount.

Use these statements to write two simultaneous equations and solve them.
Show your working.

$p =$ .... $q =$ ....

10 Andy and Carol are out walking. They reach a field where a sign says 'Beware of the bull!'. Instead of walking across the field, they decide to walk around the edge.

The field is rectangular with a width of 25 m and a length of 42 m.

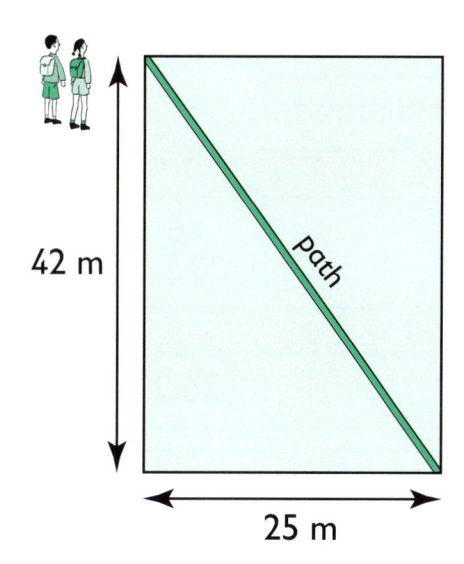

How much further do they walk around the edge than they would walk straight across the field?
Show your working. Give your answer to 2 significant figures.

Mental Maths Test
Answer Sheet

5-second questions

| 1 | 3.4 ✗ | 3/4 |

| 2 | 25 ✓ | 23   27 |

| 3 | 60000 ✓ |

| 4 | ✗   millilitres |

| 5 | 2/3 ✓ | 16/24 |

| 6 | 3.627 ✗ | 36.27 |

10-second questions

| 7 | p = 5 ✗ | 2p = q |

| 8 | 14 ✗ % |

| 9 | 20 cm² ✓ | 5 cm, 8 cm |

| 10 | |

TOTAL

Mental Maths Test – Answer sheet

11	✗	8.32
12	5.6 10/12 ✓	5/6
13	centimetres ✗	
14	9 × 8 = 36 ✓	2y = 9
15	8 ✗	
16	1.42 ✓	1.4 1.59 1.6 1.42
17	14 ✗	4a + 3b 8a + 6b
18	1 ✓	−3 < s < 2

15-second questions

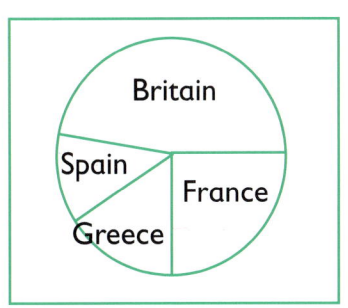

19	5 and 6 ✗	
20	50 ✓	(pie chart: Britain, Spain, France, Greece)

TOTAL 10

35

Mental Maths Test – Answer sheet

21   24 ✗

22   11913 ✓

23   32 × 1.6 = 5.12 ✗   32 × 16 = 512

24 ✗   area = n^2

25   £ 7.45 ✓

26 ✗

27 $3^2 + 8$ 4^2 $2^3 + 2^3$ ✓

28   metres ✗   2w, w, Perimeter = 18 metres

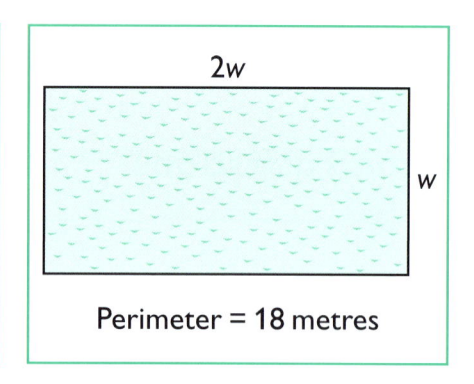

29 ✗

30 ✗ $y - 4 = z$

12/30

TOTAL 10

Maths Test Answers

Paper 1

Question number	Answer	Mark	Comments and tips
Practice questions	208 795 28 42		You cannot use calculators for *any* of the questions in Paper 1. You can work answers out anywhere on the page or you can work answers out mentally. For some questions you might gain a mark for your written working out even if you get the answer wrong.
Calculations			
1a b c d e	100 6 128 60 Two numbers to make equation true e.g. 55, 5.	5	Always look at the finished equation when you have written a missing number to see if it makes sense. For the question ☐ – 50 = 78, if you <u>incorrectly</u> took away 50 from 78 and wrote the missing number 28, you can see that 28 – 50 doesn't equal 78!
Shape symmetry			
2	Shape B 0 2 Shape C 3 3 Shape D 0 1 Shape E 5 5 1 mark is given for each shape.	4	A useful thing to remember is that for regular shapes (those with sides and angles the same size) the number of lines of symmetry and order of rotational symmetry are the same as the number of sides. Look at shapes A, C and E. They are regular shapes.
Fractions			
3a	$\frac{3}{10}$	1	The stick is divided into ten equal parts (the number on the bottom of your fraction) and the cane is as long as 3 parts (the number on the top).
3b	$\frac{3}{5}$	1	This question specifies giving your answer in its simplest form. Cane B is as long as six-tenths. $\frac{6}{10} = \frac{3}{5}$ To simplify fractions, cancel the top and bottom numbers by the same number, in this case by 2.
3c	80%	1	Eight-tenths as a percentage is 80%. If you think of the whole stick as 100%, each part is one-tenth (10%) so eight parts are 80%.
3d	40 cm	1	$\frac{2}{5}$ is the same value as four-tenths. Four-tenths of a metre is 40 cm.
3e	300 cm or 3 m	1	Ten pieces of Cane A measuring 30 cm each would be 300 cm or 3 m.
3f	Cane E is longer than Cane B but shorter than Cane C.	1	$\frac{2}{3}$ of a metre is 66.6 cm. Cane B is 60 cm and Cane C is 80 cm.

Maths Test Answers – Paper 1

Question number	Answer	Mark	Comments and tips
Money			
4a	£123 or £123.00	1	Note that amounts should never be written with both the **£** sign and a **p** sign, e.g. £123.00p.
4b	£600	1	
4c	£9.50	1	
4d	£11.52	1	To check an answer like this while sitting the paper, try adding the amount Leroy spends to the answer you have written. It should come to £20.
4e	£15.80	1	
Probability			
5a	$\frac{1}{12}$	1	There are 12 coins. The probability of picking the 1p coin is one out of twelve.
5b	*(mark on number line between 0 and 1, at midpoint)*	1	The probability of picking a 20p coin is six out of twelve. This is the same as one-half.
5c	*(mark on number line between 0 and 1, near 1)*	1	There are 12 coins. The probability of picking a 5p coin is $\frac{2}{12}$ so the probability of not getting a 5p is $\frac{10}{12}$. Note that $\frac{10}{12}$ is the same as $\frac{5}{6}$.
5d	*(mark on number line between 0 and 1, at 11/12)*	1	The probability of picking a silver coin is $\frac{11}{12}$ as only the 1p is not silver.
5e	Your explanation should include the idea that tests are not always reliable. Davina only tried it 60 times. The probability of picking a 5p is still $\frac{2}{12}$ and the probability of picking a 10p is $\frac{3}{12}$.	1	The greater the number of tests carried out, the more likely the results will match the theoretical probability.
Using letters			
6a	$n + 4$	1	
6b	$n \div 2$ or $\frac{1}{2}n$ or $\frac{n}{2}$	1	Any of these three expressions are acceptable, but the second two are preferable.

40

Maths Test Answers – Paper 1

Question number	Answer	Mark	Comments and tips
6c	2*n*	1	The answers *n* × 2 or 2 × *n* are acceptable, but it is better to shorten the expression to 2*n*.
6d	20*n*	1	The answers *n* × 20 or 20 × *n* are acceptable, but it is better to shorten the expression to 20*n*.
6e	The fish tanks do not hold the same amount. Your explanation should show that 3(*n* – 3) becomes 3*n* – 9 when the brackets are removed.	1	When removing brackets you must multiply whatever is outside the brackets by everything inside the brackets. People sometimes forget and only multiply the first number in the brackets. 3(*n* – 3) does NOT equal 3*n* – 3, but 3*n* – **9**.
Sequences			
7a	15 21 49 100 1 mark for each correct row.	2	The number of coloured squares is always 1 more than the shape number doubled. The number of white squares is always the shape number squared.
7b	2*n* + 1 (or equivalent expression) n^2 or *n* × *n* 1 mark for each correct row.	2	The number of coloured squares is always 1 more than the shape number (*n*) doubled = 2*n* + 1. The number of white squares is always the shape number squared: n^2.
7c	$n^2 + 2n + 1$	1	
7d	Set 2	1	A tip for finding the correct set in a question of this type is to look at the number multiplied by *n*, in this case 2. Look for the set of shapes which grows by 2 each time.
Angles			
8	*a* = 50° *b* = 30° *c* = 150°	3	Angle *a* is found by subtracting 130° from 180° (angles on a straight line). The angles inside a triangle add to 180°. The third (unmarked) angle is 20° (from angles on a straight line) and 130 + 20 = 150, which means that *b* must be 30°. Angle *c* is found by subtracting *b* (30°) from 180°.
Linear equations			
9a	*y* = 7	1	Lines with the equation *y* = 'a number' are horizontal. Lines with the equation *x* = 'a number' are vertical. Lines with an equation with *x* and *y* are diagonal.

41

Maths Test Answers – Paper 1

Question number	Answer	Mark	Comments and tips
9b	$y = x + 3$	1	In the general equation $y = mx + c$, m stands for the gradient. For this line, the gradient (slope) is the same as the line AB which is given as 1. The c stands for the point at which the line would cross the y axis. The line AB crosses at 7; the line you are finding, CD, crosses at 3.
9c	A diagonal line should be drawn, passing through the co-ordinates (0, 10) and (10, 0).	1	This equation can be rearranged to form the equation $x + y = 10$. You can see that if x is 0, $y = 10$ and when $x = 1$, $y = 9$ etc. These points can be plotted on the graph to form the line.
Areas			
10a	2 cm	2	Remember to look at the formula sheet at the beginning of the test to help you with questions of this type. 1 mark given for using the equation area = $\frac{(a + b) \times h}{2}$ even if answer is incorrect. The area of the parallelogram is 4.5 cm^2 so the area of the trapezium is therefore 13.5 cm^2. $13.5 = \frac{(4 + 9.5) \times h}{2}$ $13.5 = \frac{13.5 \times h}{2}$ Here you can see that if 13.5 divided by 2 and multiplied by h is 13.5, h must be 2.
10b	Area = $12y^2$	1	Area = $\frac{(2y + 6y) \times 3y}{2}$ = $\frac{8y}{2} \times 3y$ = $4y \times 3y$ = $12y^2$

Maths Test Answers
Paper 2

Question number	Answer	Mark	Comments and tips
Running rates			
1a	26 40 14 40 58 18	2	Score 1 mark for each row. Each interval on the vertical axis is worth 2 m.
1b	Your explanation should include the fact that Dev runs at a fairly a steady rate, whereas Ben starts more slowly and speeds up, but slows down again near the end.	2	
1c	Ben	1	You can see on the graph that Ben has reached the 60 m line at 8 s.
Square sequences			
2a	Your explanation should show that you have noticed that the two central coloured squares in each shape are represented by $+2$ and the $3n$ represents the three 'legs' on each shape.	1	Notice that the number of coloured squares remains constant and the number of white squares grows. The parts that grow are represented in the expression by a number of n. The constant squares, such as the coloured ones, are represented by just a number.
2b	36 and 2	2	The rule is $3n + 2$. For shape 12, $n = 12$ so $3n + 2 = (3 \times 12) + 2 = 36$ and 2.
2c	20	1	The rule is $3n + 2$. If $3n + 2 = 62$, then $3n = 62 - 2 = 60$. If $3n = 60$, then n must be 20.
2d	$4n + 1$	1	There is 1 central coloured square (+1) and 4 'legs' ($4n$), so the total number is $4n + 1$. The equations $1 + 4n$ or $(4 \times n) + 1$ are also acceptable.
Cubes			
3a	A cuboid accurately drawn, e.g. with 3 coloured cubes positioned.	2	The cube can be drawn in a different orientation. Only 1 mark if coloured cubes are not correctly correctly shaded.

43

Maths Test Answers – Paper 2

Question number	Answer	Mark	Comments and tips
3b	2 cm, 2 cm, 2 cm	1	
3c	48 cm^3	2	The volume of a cuboid is found by multiplying the length by the width by the height: $3 \times 4 \times 4 = 48$ cm^3.
3d	4	1	
3e	$\frac{44}{48}$ or $\frac{22}{24}$ or $\frac{11}{12}$	1	If four cannot be seen then 44 (48 minus 4) can be seen. 44 out of a total of 48 is written as a fraction as $\frac{44}{48}$.
Equations			
4	$x = 2.6$ cm	4	This requires a 'trial and error method'. The result should be checked by putting the value of x into the equation.
Ratio			
5a	100 g	1	The ratio is 2 parts butter for every 7 parts flour. We can write this as the ratio 2:7. If there is 350 g of flour (fifty times the number in the ratio) then butter must be fifty times the other number in the ratio, i.e. $2 \times 50 = 100$.
5b	280 g	1	The ratio is 2:7. If there is 80 g of butter (forty times the number in the ratio) then flour must be forty times the other number in the ratio, i.e. $7 \times 40 = 280$.
5c	1400 g flour and 400 g butter 1 mark each	2	In the ratio 2:7, there is a total of 9 parts. If a total of 1800 g is mixed (200 times the ratio total) then both butter and flour must be 200 times their numbers in the ratio.
Scalene triangle			
6a	To check your answer, measure the perpendicular height of your triangle. If the height is exactly 2.8 cm then you score 2 marks. If the height is between 2.6 cm and 3 cm, you score 1 mark.	2	
6b	22° or 23°	1	
Area and circumference			
7a	200.96 cm^2 or 201 cm^2 Only 1 mark for the answer 201.06 cm^2 (use of π button on calculator).	2	Area of a circle = πr^2. The radius is half the diameter $(16 \div 2) = 8$ Area = $64 \times \pi = 64 \times 3.14$ NOTE: *If you have used the π button on your calculator your answer will be different. The question stated that π should be taken as 3.14.*

Maths Test Answers – Paper 2

Question number	Answer	Mark	Comments and tips
7b	11 cm	2	The circumference of a circle is $2\pi r$ or πd. If the circumference is 69, then divide 69 by π to find the diameter and then halve to find r.
Sports results			
8a	110	1	Add together 2, 19, 38, 32, 14 and 5.
8b	This graph does not give enough information about the precise distances the students threw.	1	Within the distance 20–29 m, the students could have thrown over 25 m, in which case Serena is wrong, or under 25 m, in which case she is right.
8c	Again, we need more information.	1	The range of a set of data is found by subtracting the lowest value from the highest value.
8d	29.2 m 1 mark for 29.227 m or 29.23 m.	2	The total values for fx should be divided by 110 (the number of students) to find the mean value.
Simultaneous equations			
9	$p = 4$ $q = 6$ 1 mark for each. 2 marks for these equations shown: $4p + 2 = 3q$ $8p - 2 = 5q$	4	There are different methods for solving simultaneous equations. One example is shown below: Double each value in the equation $4p + 2 = 3q$ to give $8p + 4 = 6q$. Subtract $8p - 2 = 5q$ from this equation to get $6 = q$, therefore Emily has £6. If $q = 6$, then $4p + 2 = 3 \times 6 = 18$. Thus $4p + 2 = 18$ and $4p = 16$, so p must be 4.
Field			
10	18 m 3 marks if your working shows the number 48.877 or 49 but the answer is wrong, or if your answer has more than 2 digits, e.g. 18.12. Score 2 marks for the number 2389 in your working.	4	Let x be the length of the path. Use Pythagoras' Theorem ($a^2 + b^2 = c^2$). $42^2 + 25^2 = x^2$ so $x^2 = 2389$, therefore $x = 48.877$ m. Once the distance across the field has been found, add the distances 42 m and 25 m to get 67 m. This value is how far they walked. The difference between 67 m and 48.877 m is 18.123 m, which is 18 m to 2 significant figures.

Mental Maths Test
Answers

1. 0.75
2. 25
3. 60 000
4. 3000
5. $\frac{2}{3}$
6. 36.3
7. 2.5
8. 70%
9. 20 cm^2
10. 20
11. any two numbers that add to 8.32 e.g. 8.0 + 0.32
12. any fraction equivalent to five-sixths e.g. $\frac{10}{12}$
13. 27 cm
14. 36
15. 13
16. 1.42
17. 24
18. any value larger than -3 and less than 2 e.g. -1
19. 4 and 9
20. 50
21. $\frac{3}{16}$
22. any three odd numbers that add to 33 e.g. 25, 5 and 3
23. 51.2
24. $4n$
25. £7.45
26. 19
27. $3^2 + 8$
28. 6 m
29. 8
30. $y - 2 = z + 2$

National Curriculum Levels

Write your scores below.

Mark scored in Paper 1 ⬜ out of 45

Mark scored in Paper 2 ⬜ out of 45

Mark scored in Mental Maths Test ⬜ 12 out of 30

Total score ⬜ out of 120

Use this table to find what level you might be working at.

Mark	0–16	17–32	33–65	66–100	101–110	111–120
Level	Level 3	Level 4	Level 5	Level 6	Level 7	Level 8

If you need more practice in any Maths topics, use the WHSmith Key Stage 3 Maths Revision Guide.

English

English at Key Stage 3

The SATs tests for Key Stage 3 now complement the Key Stage 3 national strategy: the *Framework for Teaching English*. The Writing Test links with the word-level, sentence-level and text-level structure of the *Framework for Teaching*, and the Reading Test requires pupils to show their understanding of how texts work.

All pupils in their final year of Key Stage 3 must be assessed. The English Tests assess levels 4–7 of the National Curriculum. (Pupils who have been assessed as working at level 3 or below in English do not have to have their tests 'disapplied', as teacher assessment is the sole statutory requirement for pupils working at this level.)

In English pupils are required to sit three test papers.

Paper	Times	Content and marks	NC levels assessed
Reading	75 minutes, including 15 minutes' reading time	Based upon three texts. Approximately 15 questions (32 marks)	Levels 4–7
Writing	45 minutes, including 15 minutes' planning time	One writing task (30 marks)	Levels 4–7
Shakespeare	75 minutes Writing 30 minutes Reading and Understanding 45 minutes	Writing (20 marks) Reading and Understanding (18 marks)	Levels 4–7

English at Key Stage 3

The Reading paper

- This paper will include three texts. These will range across genre and can be literary, non-literary, fiction and non-fiction.
- They will be linked according to theme.
- The reading test lasts 60 minutes.
- Pupils will be given 15 minutes reading time on top of this.
- There will be about 15 questions which are varied in format.
- These will take into account people's different learning styles.
- These questions will be linked to the assessment focuses for reading.
- They will also link to word-, sentence- and text-level objectives of the Key Stage 3 national strategy.
- Not all questions are of equal difficulty, but the mark scheme will be obvious. There are 32 marks in total.

The Writing paper

Writing ability is assessed using two written tasks – one longer and one shorter.

The shorter one will be on the Shakespeare paper.

Pupils will be required to complete them both. The tasks will focus on:

- different purposes
- different forms of writing.

Planning formats will be provided in both cases.

The Writing paper (the longer writing task) will last 45 minutes. 15 minutes extra is provided for planning.

It is worth 30 marks in total.

Information is given about audience and purpose and usually about the form and the level of formality required in the writing.

The examiners require a piece of continuous writing, narrative or non-narrative.

It will be marked according to three sets of criteria:

- sentence structure and punctuation (8 marks)
- text structure and organisation (8 marks)
- composition and effect (14 marks).

Shakespeare

The Shakespeare paper is 75 minutes long.

Section A is the shorter writing task. Pupils are given 30 minutes for this. It is worth 20 marks. Note that 4 marks are allocated for spelling. One writing task is set on each of the three plays (see page 50). Each writing task relates to the themes of the play studied. A planning format is not included, but information will be provided about the audience, purpose and structure of the piece. This piece is assessed on the quality of the writing, not necessarily on the understanding of the play.

English at Key Stage 3

Section B is the Shakespeare task for Reading and Understanding. This will last 45 minutes. It is worth **18** marks. One question only will be set on each play. The question will test understanding of character, themes, language and dramatic conventions. The answer will be assessed only for understanding of the play and for how pupils respond to its literary merits. It will not be assessed for written expression. The task will concentrate on the detailed study of two sections of one of the three designated Shakespeare plays for the year. The passages will be printed on the exam paper. For 2004 these are:

Henry V
Twelfth Night
Macbeth

Marking the papers

SATs papers are marked by external examiners according to a strict set of criteria set by the Qualifications and Curriculum Authority. In this way a national consensus can be achieved which is much fairer to all candidates. Each pupil is awarded a final score for the whole English test. This will equate to a National Curriculum level.

For guidelines on marking these practice papers, see pages 70–77.

Each paper has a series of 'assessment focuses'.

Reading assessment focuses

Among the most important are:

- Describe, select and retrieve information
- Deduce, infer and interpret information
- Comment on organisation and structure (including grammar and presentation)
- Comment on a writer's use of language (including literary features at word and sentence level)
- Comment on a writer's purpose and attitude and their effect on the reader
- Relate texts to contexts, e.g. historical or cultural, as well as literary traditions.

Writing assessment focuses

Among the most important are:

- Write imaginative, interesting texts
- Write appropriately to topic, audience and purpose
- Organise and structure texts appropriately
- Write and construct coherent paragraphs
- Write clear and varied sentences for effect
- Write with technical accuracy, using appropriate grammar and punctuation
- Select appropriate vocabulary
- Spell words correctly.

English at Key Stage 3

Tips for success at Key Stage 3

- Look at the entire test paper first to establish what has to be done. Highlight the time restraints and the number of questions which need to be answered.
- Pace yourself – keep an eye on the clock.
- Read the questions carefully. Underline key words, e.g. 'compare', 'two reasons …'. Be relevant in your answers.
- Avoid getting too involved with any one question. You may have a great deal to say about it, but it will only be worth a set number of marks.
- Follow the help given on the paper. If the examiners have given a list of points to follow then use these as the plan for your work.
- Make notes on the test paper. Underline important points, circle or highlight information relevant to the question.
- Back up points you make with short quotations from the passage.
- If you get stuck on a question, leave it for the moment – but remember to leave space in your answer book in case you want to go back.
- Your basic English is important – you need to communicate what you know and understand. Look carefully for those words you always spell incorrectly!
- If you have time left, go back over your answers.

Advice for parents

Tests and exams can be very stressful. This is mostly because people do not like to feel 'judged' by others – especially if they feel that the results may not be as good as others expect!

The tests in this book are modelled as closely as possible on the 'real thing' so pupils will not be surprised by the test format. However, parents can help with the pressure of the tests by using the material in this book as a resource for teaching and learning. Do not just sit a child down with the test and tell him or her to 'get on with it'; share the experiences, questions and discussion that arises from the tests. Try sitting one yourself!

- Talk about each of the questions and possible ways forward. At this stage, discussion will be more useful than 'writing'.
- Choose a comfortable environment in which to do the tests together.
- Mark the work together, praising positive points as well as pointing out things which are not correct.
- Look closely at how the incorrect responses can be corrected, what needs to be learned or changed and how this can be done realistically. It is useful to list just two or three things which need to be done or learned before the next test session.
- Stick to the time limits – but do not insist that the entire test paper has to be completed at one go.
- Give immediate feedback – do not wait too long to discuss the performance of the candidate.
- Be positive about achievements!
- Guide your child back to school in order to ask the professional – the teacher – the person who knows most about the teaching of each pupil.

English Test: Reading Paper

Passage 3

This text is an extract from a scientific journal on a website.

http://www.jr2.ox.ac.uk/bandolier/band34/b34-5.html

A study reported in 1974 on the value of giving budgerigars to old people. The authors started with the premise that old people can suffer from periods of social isolation which can lead to substantial psychiatric deterioration. While they knew of some substantial work on the beneficial effect of pets on all ages, they were unaware of controlled studies, so they did one.

Budgerigars and begonias

There were five groups, but with only six old people aged between 75 and 81 years in each. Each elderly person was interviewed by a psychologist and a social worker, and were asked a series of 22 questions about their life and attitude. Questions like "Do you have feelings of being fed up?" and "Do you feel time drags?" Favourable rapport was established by allowing each old person to choose a small gift, like a torch or a tray.

At this stage five interventions were set up:

1. Give a budgerigar, cage, tray and bird food to six people who had a TV set.
2. Give a begonia to six people who had a TV set.
3. Give a budgerigar, cage, tray and bird food to six people who had no TV set.
4. Give a begonia to six people who had no TV set.
5. Control group of six people, half of whom had a TV set.

The questionnaire was administered again, five months later, and items were marked as no change, favourable change or unfavourable change.

However, there were some problems:

- Six of 18 old people refused a budgerigar – mainly because they didn't like seeing birds in cages. None of the old people offered a begonia refused.
- Some of the budgerigars died within six weeks of placement – but most of the subjects either had another bird given them or bought one themselves.
- At the time of the follow up visit only just over half of the old people could be assessed. Some had died, some had moved, and some just couldn't be contacted. So analysis was on half the original number of subjects.

Results

All 12 old people who had budgerigars had given the birds names, and insisted on making arrangements for food and so on. Some had made elaborate playgrounds and many taught the birds to speak. It was not reported whether similar attention was given to the begonias. Having or not having a TV set made no difference, and we have combined the data from the questionnaire scores. At five months the controls had an overall unfavourable change in questionnaire scores, people given begonias had no overall change, but those given budgerigars had dramatically favourable changes in questionnaire scores.

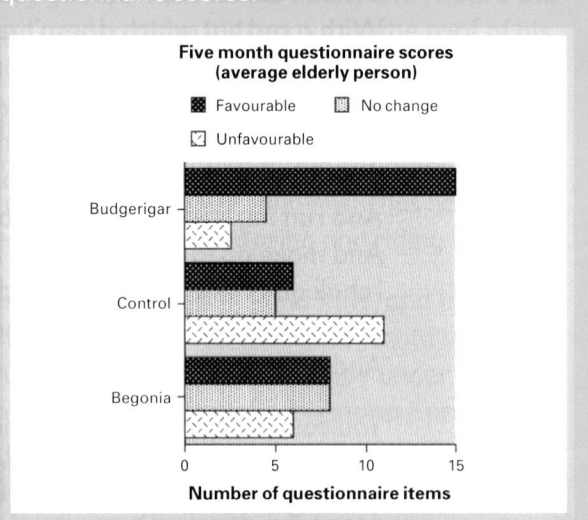

Comment

This trial was neither randomised, nor did it have particularly large numbers. It did show a big effect and tried hard to establish that the fact of the trial did not confound the effect of the budgerigar. The authors comment that it wasn't always so much the budgerigar itself, but the focus it made for discussion during social visits. For some of the elderly people the budgerigar stimulated visits, from local children, for instance, who came to teach the bird their names.

English Test: Reading Paper

Questions 1–5 are about *Dylan Thomas's autobiography*

1. Write what you learn about the character of the old man and how he explains what he is doing. (2 marks)
   Focus: Deduce, infer and interpret information and events or ideas from the text.

2. What does the author suggest when he describes the old man 'trotting his tongue on the roof of his mouth' and 'his tongue had powerful hooves'? (2 marks)
   Focus: Comment on the writer's use of language, grammatical and literary features (word and sentence level).

3. Find and quote two examples to show the noises the boy did not like in the house. (1 mark)
   Focus: Describe, select and retrieve information and events or ideas from the text. Use quotation and reference to the text.

4. Comment on the effectiveness of the following: i.e., show what the descriptions add to the author's intention in the passage.

   As loudly as a bull with a megaphone…
   His pipe smouldered among his whiskers like a little burning hayrick on a stick … (3 marks)
   Focus: Comment on the writer's use of language, grammatical and literary features (word and sentence level).

5. Show how the writer effectively creates the old man's fantasy. (4 marks)
   You should write about:
   - The changing attitude of the boy towards his grandfather.
   - How the boy becomes aware of what is happening and what he had been doing previously.
   - What the house is like.
   - What he hears and sees as he gets closer to the room.
   - What his grandfather's fantasy is and how the old man is dramatising this.
   - The unusual images and description used by the writer.

   Focus: Identify and comment on the writer's purposes and viewpoints and the effect of the text on the reader.

Questions 6–10 are about *Warning*

6. Find and quote a phrase from the poem which shows that the author is looking forward to a time when she is old. (1 mark)
   Focus: Describe, select and retrieve information and events or ideas from the text. Use quotation and reference to the text.

7. List four things which the poet says she will be able to do when she is old. (2 marks)
   Focus: Describe, select and retrieve information, events or ideas from the text. Use quotation and reference to the text.

8. Explain how the poet contrasts what people expect of an old lady with how she would like to behave.

   In your answer you should comment on:
   - What the poem says in the final section about what is expected.
   - How the earlier images contrast with this.
   - How the writer feels about this.
   - How the reader feels about this. (2 marks)

   Focus: Deduce, infer and interpret information and events or ideas from the text.

English Test: Reading Paper

9 The poet uses the verb 'gobble',

And gobble up samples in shops.

Comment on how well you think the verb works in the characterisation of the woman. **(2 marks)**

Focus: Comment on the writer's use of language, grammatical and literary features (word and sentence level).

10 The definition of someone who is 'eccentric' is: 'not following the established pattern of conduct; odd'. Explain whether you think the lady is this poem deserves this description.

In your answer you should comment on:

- What you expect the established 'pattern of conduct' might be for a lady such as the one in the poem.
- What she would like to do and why.
- How you feel about this. **(5 marks)**

Focus: Identify and comment on the writer's purposes and viewpoints and the effect of the text on the reader.

Questions 11–15 are about *the scientific journal website*

11 What did the researchers think would be the benefit of giving old people budgerigars or begonias? **(1 mark)**

Focus: Describe, select and retrieve information and events or ideas from the text. Use quotation and reference to the text.

12 Find and quote a sentence from the passage which explains how the researchers managed to create good relationships with the old people. **(1 mark)**

Focus: Describe, select and retrieve information and events or ideas from the text. Use quotation and reference to the text.

13 What is meant by 'five interventions were set up' and why do you think these were necessary? **(2 marks)**

Focus: Deduce, infer and interpret information and events or ideas from the text.

14 Explain what the value of the graph could be in this kind of writing and what other organisational and design features help to make the explanation clearer. **(2 marks)**

Focus: Comment on the structure and organisation of texts, grammatical and presentational features (text level).

15 Explain the impact on the meaning of the sentences, of the words in bold in the two examples. **(2 marks)**

| The questionnaire was administered again, five months later, and items were marked as no change, favourable change or unfavourable change. **However,** there were some problems … | At five months the controls had an overall unfavourable change in questionnaire scores, people given begonias had no overall change, **but** those given budgerigars had dramatically favourable changes in questionnaire scores. |

Focus: Comment on the writer's use of language, grammatical and literary features (word and sentence level).

English Test
Writing Paper

- The paper is 45 minutes long, including 15 minutes' planning time.
- There is one task which has 30 marks.
- Plan your work on the planning format.

> Some say that respect for the older generation is disappearing. Imagine that you work for an organisation which aims to help old people lead a fuller life in our society. Write a report about this, suggesting ways of changing the attitudes of young people.
>
> In your answer you should:
>
> - Use the appropriate style for a report.
> - Give your views with evidence or stories to back this up.
> - Provide a few sensible and developed strategies for change.

Planning format

Introduction: What is the subject of the report?	Description of the issue
Examples	What can be done? Examples?
Language issues: paragraphs easy to follow, include facts and opinions, mainly present tense	Conclusion

57

English Test
Shakespeare

Preparing for the Shakespeare play test

There's only one way to prepare for answering questions on a Shakespeare play – read the play! Watching the video is not good enough!

In your test, you will be asked to deal with one aspect of the play you have studied in relation to one or two scenes, but you must also be prepared to share your knowledge of the rest of the play by putting certain aspects of the play into context and saying what has happened before – and if anything has changed – and even what will happen later in the play.

Remember: Do not write everything you know about the play – you are not being tested on how good your memory is – and answer the question you have been set, not the one you want to be set!

Draft your answer before you finally write it:

- Take time to think about what information you need from the scenes printed for you.
- Spend at least 15 minutes reading the scenes carefully.
- Do not be afraid to underline or circle important quotations. Write notes in the margin as you go along.
- Use the helpful pointers given to you on the question paper and write notes on each section. Prove each of your points with a brief quotation.
- Take each of the pointers in turn and think about how to join them together as paragraphs later on. You could even number them in your notes – just to ensure that you do not miss out any.
- Do not write out huge sections from the play. The examiner wants to know what and how you write – not how Shakespeare did!

It is important that you time yourself effectively. You need to pace yourself. You have time to read and annotate the scene printed for you and time to draft and write your answer. You will not be given extra time.

You are being assessed in this section on your knowledge and awareness of the Shakespeare play you have studied – its plot, ideas, the characters and why they behave in the way that they do, the language and even the staging of the scene. But remember, you will also have to write clearly to communicate these ideas. Hence marks are allocated for use of appropriate style, clarity and organisation of writing, spelling, grammar and punctuation, so leave enough time to check your work. Your handwriting is also important.

Henry V
Shakespeare

- The paper is **1 hour 15 minutes** long.
- It has two sections.
- Section A assesses your writing and has 20 marks.
- Section B assesses your reading and understanding of *Henry V*, and has 18 marks.
- You should spend about 30 minutes on Section A.
- You should spend about 45 minutes on Section B.

Section A: Writing

You should spend about 30 minutes on this section.

Henry V is a play about the nature of kingship.

> There is a debate at the moment about whether the monarchy is an outmoded institution.
>
> You are asked to take part in a debate arguing either for or against the institution of monarchy and its usefulness to young people today.
>
> This presentation is to be in the form of a speech.

Write the speech.

20 marks including 4 marks for spelling.

> **Remember:**
>
> The aim of this is to persuade.
> State your opinions briefly and back up each one with evidence.
> Think about your spelling. There are marks awarded for this.

English Test: Shakespeare

Section B: Reading and Understanding

You should spend about 45 minutes on this section.

> Read the excerpts from Act 3 Scene 1 and 2, Act 4 Scene 7.
>
> In the early part of *Henry V*, people express doubts that the 'madcap Prince of Wales' could become a brave and patriotic king.
>
> Patriotism is a major theme of *Henry V*. Explain what these two scenes show about the development of Henry into a great British king.
>
> Support your ideas by referring to the printed extracts.

18 marks

Before you write you should decide:

- Why he can make the claim to the throne.
- What obstacles stand in his way.
- Why he personally wants to succeed.
- What happens in France to prove he is a great patriotic king.

Read the task again before you begin to write your answer.

> **EXAMINER'S TIPS**
>
> Remind yourself about some of the following points.
>
> Set the scene in the context of the rest of the play. Henry has to go to France to fight as he must prove himself to the British that he is no longer the 'madcap prince' of his youth. He has given up his friends from the tavern and is proving a brave and strong king. He defeats the French at Harfleur and stands in contrast with the Dauphin as being more interested in his people and his country than in mere appearance.
>
> At the battle of Agincourt the British are wildly outnumbered, 'five to one', and they have been fighting in France for a long time. All the odds are against them.
>
> Henry appeals to the patriotism of his men. Theirs will be a special group. Those who fight will become the stuff of legend in England. He appeals to 'honour' and the sense of chivalry – hence to their fear of cowardice.

English Test: Shakespeare

Henry V

Act 3 Scene 1 and 2

KING HENRY V … Now set the teeth and stretch the nostril wide,
Hold hard the breath and bend up every spirit
To his full height. On, on, you noblest English.
Whose blood is fet from fathers of war-proof!
Fathers that, like so many Alexanders,
Have in these parts from morn till even fought
And sheathed their swords for lack of argument:
Dishonour not your mothers; now attest
That those whom you call'd fathers did beget you.
Be copy now to men of grosser blood,
And teach them how to war. And you, good yeoman,
Whose limbs were made in England, show us here
The mettle of your pasture; let us swear
That you are worth your breeding; which I doubt not;
For there is none of you so mean and base,
That hath not noble lustre in your eyes.
I see you stand like greyhounds in the slips,
Straining upon the start. The game's afoot:
Follow your spirit, and upon this charge
Cry 'God for Harry, England, and Saint George!'

[Exeunt. Alarum, and chambers go off]

SCENE II. The same.

[Enter NYM, BARDOLPH, PISTOL, and Boy]

BARDOLPH On, on, on, on, on! to the breach, to the breach!

NYM Pray thee, corporal, stay: the knocks are too hot; and, for mine own part, I have not a case of lives: the humour of it is too hot, that is the very plain-song of it.

PISTOL The plain-song is most just: for humours do abound:
Knocks go and come; God's vassals drop and die;
And sword and shield,
In bloody field,
Doth win immortal fame.

Boy Would I were in an alehouse in London! I would give all my fame for a pot of ale and safety.

PISTOL And I:
If wishes would prevail with me,
My purpose should not fail with me,
But thither would I hie.

Boy As duly, but not as truly,
As bird doth sing on bough.

[Enter FLUELLEN]

FLUELLEN Up to the breach, you dogs! avaunt, you cullions!

[Driving them forward]

PISTOL Be merciful, great duke, to men of mould.
Abate thy rage, abate thy manly rage,
Abate thy rage, great duke!
Good bawcock, bate thy rage; use lenity, sweet chuck!

English Test: Shakespeare

Act 4 Scene 7

[Alarum. Enter KING HENRY, and forces; WARWICK, GLOUCESTER, EXETER, and others]

KING HENRY V I was not angry since I came to France
Until this instant. Take a trumpet, herald;
Ride thou unto the horsemen on yon hill:
If they will fight with us, bid them come down,
Or void the field; they do offend our sight:
If they'll do neither, we will come to them,
And make them skirr away, as swift as stones
Enforced from the old Assyrian slings:
Besides, we'll cut the throats of those we have,
And not a man of them that we shall take
Shall taste our mercy. Go and tell them so.

[Enter MONTJOY]

EXETER Here comes the herald of the French, my liege.

GLOUCESTER His eyes are humbler than they used to be.

KING HENRY V How now! what means this, herald? know'st thou not
That I have fined these bones of mine for ransom?
Comest thou again for ransom?

MONTJOY No, great king:
I come to thee for charitable licence,
That we may wander o'er this bloody field
To look our dead, and then to bury them;
To sort our nobles from our common men.
For many of our princes—woe the while!—
Lie drown'd and soak'd in mercenary blood;
So do our vulgar drench their peasant limbs
In blood of princes; and their wounded steeds
Fret fetlock deep in gore and with wild rage
Yerk out their armed heels at their dead masters,
Killing them twice. O, give us leave, great king,
To view the field in safety and dispose
Of their dead bodies!

KING HENRY V I tell thee truly, herald,
I know not if the day be ours or no;
For yet a many of your horsemen peer
And gallop o'er the field.

MONTJOY The day is yours.

KING HENRY V Praised be God, and not our strength, for it!
What is this castle call'd that stands hard by?

MONTJOY They call it Agincourt.

KING HENRY V Then call we this the field of Agincourt,
Fought on the day of Crispin Crispianus.

FLUELLEN Your grandfather of famous memory, an't please your majesty, and your great-uncle Edward the Plack Prince of Wales, as I have read in the chronicles, fought a most prave pattle here in France.

KING HENRY V They did, Fluellen.

FLUELLEN Your majesty says very true: if your majesties is remembered of it, the Welshmen did good service in a garden where leeks did grow, wearing leeks in their Monmouth caps; which, your majesty know, to this hour is an honourable badge of the service; and I do believe your majesty takes no scorn to wear the leek upon Saint Tavy's day.

KING HENRY V I wear it for a memorable honour;
For I am Welsh, you know, good countryman.

Twelfth Night
English Test: Shakespeare

- The paper is 1 hour 15 minutes long.
- It has two sections.
- Section A assesses your writing and has 20 marks.
- Section B assesses your reading and understanding of *Twelfth Night*, and has 18 marks.
- You should spend about 30 minutes on Section A.
- You should spend about 45 minutes on Section B.

Section A: Writing

You should spend about 30 minutes on this section.

In *Twelfth Night*, Malvolio is seen as the character who is against people enjoying themselves.

> Imagine you have to take on his role in a modern-day interpretation. You are given the task of preventing any enjoyment in your house. You advocate that the following should not be allowed:
> - watching TV
> - going out with friends
> - listening to music
> - eating chocolate.

Write what you are going to pin up at home as a justification of this.

20 marks including 4 for spelling.

> **Remember:**
> The aim of this is to persuade.
> State your opinions briefly and back up each one with evidence.
> Think about your spelling. There are marks awarded for this.

Section B: Reading and Understanding

You should spend about 45 minutes on this section.

> Read the excerpts from Act 2 Scene 3 and Act 4 Scene 2.
> Comedy is an important theme in *Twelfth Night*.
> Show how it is portrayed by the words and actions of the characters in these scenes and throughout the play.
> Support your ideas by referring to the printed extracts.

18 marks

Before you begin to write you should think about:
- What is amusing about what the characters say and do in the first scene?
- What is amusing about the relationship between Sir Toby and Sir Andrew?
- How does Shakespeare use irony (i.e. we know what is really happening on stage but the characters do not)?
- What is amusing about what the Clown says and why?
- What is amusing about Malvolio and how he is portrayed? How does his seriousness help the humour?
- What happens to him later as a result of this and why is this amusing? Should it be sad?
- What makes aspects of the comedy difficult for us to appreciate today? Language? Situation? Characters?

Read the task again before you begin to write your answer.

> ### EXAMINER'S TIPS
> Remind yourself about some of the following points:
> - Set the scenes in the context of the rest of the play. The first scene shows the audience how the Malvolio subplot occurs. The second scene shows us some of the results of this trick.
> - Sir Toby is fooling Sir Andrew for his money but Sir Andrew does not realise this.
> - The language is courtly – we find such word-play difficult today. The more slapstick comedy ('Go shake your ears') still appeals to us. The situation of people making fools of themselves and being tricked is a classic comedy story.
> - Malvolio is too proud and we feel that he deserves all he gets in the trick. We laugh at him but by the second scene this seems to have turned sour. Do we laugh or feel sorry for him as the trick is continued through Sir Topas?
> - The Clown proves himself to be less of a 'fool' in the intellectual content of his speech and in the way he continues the torture of Malvolio. This is a comedy but Malvolio's final words are about being revenged 'on the whole pack of you' – which does not resolve his story.

English Test: Shakespeare

Twelfth Night

Act 2 Scene 3

[Enter SIR TOBY BELCH and SIR ANDREW]

SIR TOBY BELCH	Approach, Sir Andrew: not to be abed after midnight is to be up betimes; and 'diluculo surgere,' thou know'st,—
SIR ANDREW	Nay, my troth, I know not: but I know, to be up late is to be up late.
SIR TOBY BELCH	A false conclusion: I hate it as an unfilled can. To be up after midnight and to go to bed then, is early: so that to go to bed after midnight is to go to bed betimes. Does not our life consist of the four elements?
SIR ANDREW	Faith, so they say; but I think it rather consists of eating and drinking.
SIR TOBY BELCH	Thou'rt a scholar; let us therefore eat and drink. Marian, I say! a stoup of wine!

[Enter Clown]

SIR ANDREW	Here comes the fool, i' faith.
Clown	How now, my hearts! did you never see the picture of 'we three'?
SIR TOBY BELCH	Welcome, ass. Now let's have a catch.
SIR ANDREW	By my troth, the fool has an excellent breast. I had rather than forty shillings I had such a leg, and so sweet a breath to sing, as the fool has. In sooth, thou wast in very gracious fooling last night, when thou spokest of Pigrogromitus, of the Vapians passing the equinoctial of Queubus: 'twas very good, i' faith. I sent thee sixpence for thy leman: hadst it?
Clown	I did impeticos thy gratillity; for Malvolio's nose is no whipstock: my lady has a white hand, and the Myrmidons are no bottle-ale houses.
SIR ANDREW	Excellent! why, this is the best fooling, when all is done. Now, a song.
SIR TOBY BELCH	Come on; there is sixpence for you: let's have a song.
SIR ANDREW	There's a testril of me too: if one knight give a—
Clown	Would you have a love-song, or a song of good life?
SIR TOBY BELCH	A love-song, a love-song.
SIR ANDREW	Ay, ay: I care not for good life.
Clown	*[Sings]* O mistress mine, where are you roaming? O, stay and hear; your true love's coming, That can sing both high and low: Trip no further, pretty sweeting; Journeys end in lovers meeting, Every wise man's son doth know.
SIR ANDREW	Excellent good, i' faith.

Act 4 Scene 2

MALVOLIO	Sir Topas, never was man thus wronged: good Sir Topas, do not think I am mad: they have laid me here in hideous darkness.
Clown	Fie, thou dishonest Satan! I call thee by the most modest terms; for I am one of those gentle ones that will use the devil himself with courtesy: sayest thou that house is dark?
MALVOLIO	As hell, Sir Topas.
Clown	Why it hath bay windows transparent as barricadoes, and the clearstores toward the south north are as lustrous as ebony; and yet complainest thou of obstruction?
MALVOLIO	I am not mad, Sir Topas: I say to you, this house is dark.
Clown	Madman, thou errest: I say, there is no darkness but ignorance; in which thou art more puzzled than the Egyptians in their fog.
MALVOLIO	I say, this house is as dark as ignorance, though ignorance were as dark as hell; and I say, there was never man thus abused. I am no more mad than you are: make the trial of it in any constant question.
Clown	What is the opinion of Pythagoras concerning wild fowl?
MALVOLIO	That the soul of our grandam might haply inhabit a bird.
Clown	What thinkest thou of his opinion?
MALVOLIO	I think nobly of the soul, and no way approve his opinion.
Clown	Fare thee well. Remain thou still in darkness: thou shalt hold the opinion of Pythagoras ere I will allow of thy wits, and fear to kill a woodcock, lest thou dispossess the soul of thy grandam. Fare thee well.
MALVOLIO	Sir Topas, Sir Topas!
SIR TOBY BELCH	My most exquisite Sir Topas!
Clown	Nay, I am for all waters.
MARIA	Thou mightst have done this without thy beard and gown: he sees thee not.
SIR TOBY BELCH	To him in thine own voice, and bring me word how thou findest him: I would we were well rid of this knavery. If he may be conveniently delivered, I would he were, for I am now so far in offence with my niece that I cannot pursue with any safety this sport to the upshot. Come by and by to my chamber.

[Exeunt SIR TOBY BELCH and MARIA]

Clown	[Singing] 'Hey, Robin, jolly Robin, Tell me how thy lady does.'

Macbeth
English Test: Shakespeare

- The paper is **1 hour 15 minutes** long.
- It has two sections.
- Section A assesses your writing and has **20** marks.
- Section B assesses your reading and understanding of *Macbeth*, and has **18** marks.
- You should spend about 30 minutes on Section A.
- You should spend about 45 minutes on Section B.

Section A: Writing

You should spend about 30 minutes on this section.

Macbeth is a play about kings – leaders of their states.

> Imagine you were made the leader of your school. What changes would you make and why?
>
> Write a publicity brochure advertising your new school.
>
> Would you change the buildings? The staff? The curriculum?
>
> Why?
>
> Explain the educational benefits of all you do.
>
> Which would be the most difficult decisions and why?

Write the brochure.

20 marks including 4 marks for spelling.

> **Remember:**
>
> The aim of this is to advertise and persuade.
> State your opinions briefly and back up each one with evidence.
> Think about your spelling. There are marks awarded for this.

English Test: Shakespeare

Section B: Reading and Understanding

You should spend about 45 minutes on this section.

> Read the excerpts from Act 1 Scene 3 and Act 3 Scene 1.
>
> The witches have a major impact on the story of **Macbeth**.
>
> What impact do the prophecies of the witches have on the character of Macbeth and in what way do they come true in the play?
>
> Support your ideas by referring to the printed extracts.

18 marks

Before you begin to write you should think about:

- When Macbeth met the witches previously in the play, what they told him and whether their prophecies came true.
- What he did as a result of the first prophecies he heard, and why.
- Why he has returned to the witches at this point in the play.
- How their prophecies in this scene come true later in the play.
- Their impact on the character and outcome of Macbeth.

Read the task again before you begin to write your answer.

EXAMINER'S TIPS

Remind yourself about some of the following points:

- Set the scene in the context of the rest of the play. The first scene shows 'brave Macbeth' meeting the witches, where the first of his prophecies will come true. Macbeth will rise to be king by killing all in his path so far. The witches prophesied to him at the start of the play that he would be Cawdor and king. When the first came true he was ambitious enough to believe that the second could come true. His wife's ambition pushed him.

- He feels he needs to kill Banquo because his sons will be king, and later he returns to the witches after Banquo's ghost appears to him at the banquet ('It will have blood; they say blood will have blood').

- As a result of these prophecies he kills Macduff's wife and children – giving Macduff in England the reason for personal revenge. Macbeth thinks he is invincible when he hears that no one born from a woman can kill him. Macduff later tells him that he was born by Caesarian section, and the prophecy comes true. The final warning concerns Birnham Wood coming to his castle.

- Again he thinks he is invincible – but Malcolm's army chop down branches from the wood and use them as camouflage as they approach Dunsinane Castle. Because he thinks he is invincible, Macbeth draws more into himself, locks himself away in his castle, ignores his wife's suicide and taunts his opponents as a tyrant. In the end we have lost all sympathy for him.

English Test: Shakespeare

Macbeth

Act 1 Scene 3

[Thunder. Enter the three Witches]

First Witch	Where hast thou been, sister?
Second Witch	Killing swine.
Third Witch	Sister, where thou?
First Witch	A sailor's wife had chestnuts in her lap, And munch'd, and munch'd, and munch'd:— 'Give me,' quoth I: 'Aroint thee, witch!' the rump-fed ronyon cries. Her husband's to Aleppo gone, master o' the Tiger: But in a sieve I'll thither sail, And, like a rat without a tail, I'll do, I'll do, and I'll do.
Second Witch	I'll give thee a wind.
First Witch	Thou'rt kind.
Third Witch	And I another.
First Witch	I myself have all the other, And the very ports they blow, All the quarters that they know I' the shipman's card. I will drain him dry as hay: Sleep shall neither night nor day Hang upon his pent-house lid; He shall live a man forbid: Weary se'nnights nine times nine Shall he dwindle, peak and pine: Though his bark cannot be lost, Yet it shall be tempest-tost. Look what I have.
Second Witch	Show me, show me.
First Witch	Here I have a pilot's thumb, Wreck'd as homeward he did come.

[Drum within]

Third Witch	A drum, a drum! Macbeth doth come.
ALL	The weird sisters, hand in hand, Posters of the sea and land, Thus do go about, about: Thrice to thine and thrice to mine And thrice again, to make up nine. Peace! the charm's wound up.

[Enter MACBETH and BANQUO]

MACBETH	So foul and fair a day I have not seen.

English Test: Shakespeare

Act 3 Scene 1

[Enter BANQUO]

BANQUO Thou hast it now: king, Cawdor, Glamis, all,
As the weird women promised, and, I fear,
Thou play'dst most foully for't: yet it was said
It should not stand in thy posterity,
But that myself should be the root and father
Of many kings. If there come truth from them—
As upon thee, Macbeth, their speeches shine—
Why, by the verities on thee made good,
May they not be my oracles as well,
And set me up in hope? But hush! no more.

[Sennet sounded. Enter MACBETH, as king, LADY MACBETH, as queen, LENNOX, ROSS, Lords, Ladies, and Attendants]

MACBETH Here's our chief guest.

LADY MACBETH If he had been forgotten,
It had been as a gap in our great feast,
And all-thing unbecoming.

MACBETH To-night we hold a solemn supper sir,
And I'll request your presence.

BANQUO Let your highness
Command upon me; to the which my duties
Are with a most indissoluble tie
For ever knit.

MACBETH Ride you this afternoon?

BANQUO Ay, my good lord.

MACBETH We should have else desired your good advice,
Which still hath been both grave and prosperous,
In this day's council; but we'll take to-morrow.
Is't far you ride?

BANQUO As far, my lord, as will fill up the time
'Twixt this and supper: go not my horse the better,
I must become a borrower of the night
For a dark hour or twain.

MACBETH Fail not our feast.

BANQUO My lord, I will not.

MACBETH We hear, our bloody cousins are bestow'd
In England and in Ireland, not confessing
Their cruel parricide, filling their hearers
With strange invention: but of that to-morrow,
When therewithal we shall have cause of state
Craving us jointly. Hie you to horse: adieu,
Till you return at night. Goes Fleance with you?

BANQUO Ay, my good lord: our time does call upon 's.

MACBETH I wish your horses swift and sure of foot;
And so I do commend you to their backs. Farewell.

[Exit BANQUO]

English Test: Shakespeare

                    Let every man be master of his time
                    Till seven at night: to make society
                    The sweeter welcome, we will keep ourself
                    Till supper-time alone: while then, God be with you!

[Exeunt all but MACBETH, and an attendant]

                    Sirrah, a word with you: attend those men
                    Our pleasure?

ATTENDANT   They are, my lord, without the palace gate.

English Test Answers

It is difficult to mark answers in an English test because there is often not a 'right answer' as there could be in maths. A mark scheme is provided for each question. You will need to judge how well the points made in the answer match with the score criteria. Any point should be clearly stated. Examiners should not have to 'dig' beneath the surface to find the relevant point. The most effective way of assessing work at home is to mark the piece with the candidate so both can see how the final score can be calculated. This will involve discussion of what is in the answer and what has been omitted and so can form a learning experience in itself.

It is also preferable to carry out the task yourself as a parent/carer before marking it. This will make the task clearer and it will also be interesting to see what score you achieve!

Criteria for marking

The Reading Test (marked out of 32)

The marks are allocated for each question on the paper.

The Longer Writing Task (marked out of 30)

Criteria	Marks possible	NC level
Sentence structure and punctuation	1–2 3–4 5–6 7 8	Less than 4 4 5 6 7+
Text structure and organisation	1–2 3–4 5–6 7 8	Less than 4 4 5 6 7+
Composition and effect	1–3 4–6 7–9 10–12 13–14	Less than 4 4 5 6 7+

The Shorter Writing Task (marked out of 20)

Criteria	Marks possible	NC level
Sentence structure, punctuation and text organisation	1–2 3–4 5 6	4 5 6 7+
Composition and effect	1–3 4–6 7–9 10	4 5 6 7+
Spelling	1 2 3 4	4 5 6 7+

The Shakespeare Reading Task (marked out of 18)

Marks are awarded for knowledge of the play, adopting the approach required and use of quotation.

English Test Answers
Reading Test

Questions 1–5 are about *Dylan Thomas's autobiography*

1. The fantasy of the old man goes back to a scene in the wild west. He imagines he is riding a wagon down 'a rough road'. He is dressed for the part and is totally absorbed by this activity. This seems very eccentric for an adult but some may feel that it is acceptable for an old person. Others may feel it is unacceptable for any adult. This gives us the impression of an old man who is perhaps senile; indeed the boy has been told to look after him because he may not be able to look after himself.

   However, the old man is in fact in control of all that he is doing. He is not shocked by the child's entry. He slowly stops and does not try to hide what he was doing. This would have caused more attention to be drawn to him. He has a firm grasp of young children – that they may be easily influenced by what an adult tells them but also by bribery.

   The boy does not really comprehend what is happening at first: 'Is there anything the matter, grandpa?' The image he uses of the 'ragged quilt' makes the old man seem even more in need of sympathy. However the man's strategy is very clever. He persuades the child he is having a dream. Some may feel he is a devious or sly character, but his argument is a clever one. 'Do you have nightmares boy?' He is in fact making a joke of it ('mares' are female horses) so he is enjoying the activity of getting out of the situation. Finally the old man bribes the child with money, 'Buy a cake'.

   He is not embarrassed by being 'caught'; as soon as the boy goes, he continues with his fantasy.
   (2 marks)

2. The author awakes hearing the sound of galloping horses impersonated by his grandfather. He used these two metaphors to describe how his grandfather is making the noises. They suggest the powerful noise that he is making in his fantasy.
   (2 marks)

3. 'The floorboards had creaked like mice … the walls had creaked like wood … curtains flapped and branches beaten against the window …'
   (1 mark)

4. 'As loudly as a bull with a megaphone …' The image is vaguely ridiculous but suggests the loud noise. Not only is it loud but it is amplified as if the animal had a megaphone.

   'His pipe smouldered among his whiskers like a little burning hayrick on a stick …' The image gives us some sympathy for the old man. His pipe is overflowing with tobacco and we can see the strands burning as if hay was smoking. It also suggests the shape of the tobacco ring from the bowl of his pipe.
   (3 marks)

5. The boy has been told that his grandfather is somewhat of a 'danger' – he might set the house alight because he smokes in bed. There is also a suggestion that he 'might be ill'. This gives us an impression that he is old and frail. The author obviously feels that he is somewhat eccentric – he is even a little afraid of the man: 'I felt frightened'. As a child he seems to accept the eccentric behaviour of the old man – the cowboy game the old man is playing is one that a young boy might play as well.

English Test Answers – Reading Test

The boy had been reading cowboy stories and had fallen asleep: 'I woke from a dream full of whips … windy gallops over cactus fields … roaring and riding in a book.' When he is awoken by his grandfather's noises he still thinks he is dreaming. He hears 'trotting the tongue on the roof of his mouth' – making noises like a galloping horse and other 'cowboy' noises. He sees a light under the door when he goes to investigate.

The boy is already somewhat afraid of the old eccentric house. The imagery is of creaking and 'branches beaten against the window'. He sets off in the darkness and knocks against the furniture.

When he opens the door his grandfather makes his final 'Gee-up' noise. He has been caught imagining that he is riding a wagon or a horse – 'the counterpane … his reins'. His grandfather is wearing a red waistcoat and is smoking a pipe. The old man does not stop suddenly because he has been 'caught'. He 'muffled his tongue into silence and the horses drew softly up'. He continues with the fantasy as if there is nothing wrong. He then moves through the complicated procedure of persuading the boy that he has been dreaming the whole event, but gives him some money as a bribe. As the boy leaves, the old man continues with his fantasy.

The writer makes the scene unusual by his use of imagery and description. The poet changes words into unusual verbs: 'trotting his tongue on the roof of his mouth.' The noises are described in two ways – the floorboards as mice; the mice as floorboards. The old man's tongue is animated: 'his tongue had powerful hooves.' Some of the metaphors and similes are very unusual: 'his bedroom … a great meadow', 'as loudly as a bull with a megaphone', 'like a little burning hayrick on a stick.'
(4 marks)

Questions 6–10 are about *Warning*

6 'I shall wear purple …' (future tense). 'But maybe I ought to practise a little now?'
(1 mark)

7 'wear purple …with a red hat which doesn't go … spend my pension on brandy … sit down on the pavement' (there are many more).
(2 marks)

8 The final section of the poem gives an indication of what society expects, e.g. clothes are functional – to keep her dry – not to be colourful or shocking. Her money should be spent on practical things such as paying her rent, not on making her life pleasurable in its last stages. The way she speaks is even regulated by society's expectations, e.g. she is not expected to swear. Old people are expected to set a good example to the 'younger generation' and not act in outrageous ways. However, the younger generation are permitted to do this in some ways. There is a sense that this was not always the case and this old lady seems to have 'missed out' on this. She will 'have friends to dinner'.

All the earlier images – colourful clothes, shocking activities – are seen as in direct contrast to society's 'normal' rules.

The lady is obviously not really old when she is writing the poem as she wants to 'practise' so people will not be too shocked later. There is a sense in which she has made up her mind to do some of these things.
(2 marks)

English Test Answers – Shakespeare

Twelfth Night

Key points – 2 marks for each

- The characters are amusing through what they say and what they do. The play is about how appearances can fool us and the confusion this can cause. Such situations also make comedy and the characters must add to this. Many of the characters make fools of themselves through their not being able to see through disguises or how other people feel about them. We, the audience, know what is really happening in the minds of the characters. The characters on stage only see things from their own point of view. This mismatch leads to irony, which leads to some of the cruel comedy in the play.

- The humour in the first scene is created by the relationship between Sir Andrew and Sir Toby. The audience knows that Sir Toby simply wants him for his money. Sir Andrew thinks he is being groomed to marry Olivia.

- Humour is also created by the foolishness of Sir Andrew. He thinks he is a true knight but is not. The others allow him to think this in order to make a fool of him and spend his money.

- The Clown is often seen as 'a fool' but he is one of the only people in the play who sees beyond disguise and the confusion. He is allowed to say ridiculous things, which are in fact truth. The characters take this truth from him but they would not take it from anyone else. The Clown proves himself to be less than a 'fool' in the intellectual content of his speech and in the way he continues the torture of Malvolio. – 'Fie, thou dishonest Satan!' We laugh at this, but in fact it is a very sad situation – even the others realise this at the end. This is a comedy but Malvolio's final words in the play are about being revenged on all of them, which does not resolve his story in the usual 'happy-ever-after' ending of a Shakespearean comedy.

- The first scene prepares the audience for how the Malvolio subplot occurs. The second scene shows us some of the results of this trick. Malvolio comes to spoil their fun and to stop them singing. Malvolio is too proud and we feel he deserves all he gets in the trick.

- Malvolio as a character is amusing. He shows, in the way he acts and speaks, that he thinks he is better than he is (merely Olivia's steward). The easy way he is fooled into acting stupidly is proof that he is also playing a part.

- We laugh at the trick played on Malvolio but by the second scene this seems to have turned sour. Do we laugh or feel sorry for him as the trick is continued through Sir Topas? After the trick has gone wrong for Malvolio – yellow, cross-gartered stockings and 'smiling', he is locked away as a 'lunatic' by the others. This is a further part of his humiliation. The Clown is sent to him as Sir Topas the priest – more trickery.

- The most difficult form of comedy for us today is the comedy of language, because many of the words used by Shakespeare are not known to us today. This was an intellectual comedy, very popular in the seventeenth century but less common nowadays. Visual comedy – disguise and confusion – is still popular, and we understand the situations.

- The characters are well drawn in Shakespeare, and we understand their motivation and their foibles because the same characters could exist today. The language is courtly – we find such word-play difficult today. The more slapstick comedy – 'Go shake your ears' – still appeals to us. The situation of people making fools of themselves and being tricked is a classic comedy story.

English Test Answers – Shakespeare

Macbeth

Key points – 2 marks for each

- The witches are the embodiment of evil in *Macbeth*. They prophesy the future but they cannot be said to make the events happen, 'He shall live a man forbid'. Often, they appeal to the character of Macbeth in order that he should make these things happen.

- He first meets them after the battle in this scene when they give him three prophecies: he is Thane of Glamis, he will be Thane of Cawdor and then King'. Macbeth seems to laugh at these until news arrives that the traitor Cawdor has been executed and the title given to Macbeth. If this can come true then could he not become king? Banquo is told that he will be the father of kings. He also laughs about this. This is dangerous for Banquo.

- Lady Macbeth pushes her husband into realising that it would be easy to become king. He is not ruthless enough to do this alone. Duncan comes to stay at Macbeth's castle and he is murdered. The king's sons run away in case they are blamed and Macbeth finds himself King of Scotland as prophesied, 'Thou hast it now: King, Cawdor, Glamis, all'.

- However, he wants to ensure that he will remain king and so starts his career of tyranny – killing all those who stand in his path, including Banquo – once his friend. The second scene shows Macbeth apparently inviting Banquo to a banquet when in fact he is sending him to be murdered. 'Hie you to horse: adieu, Till you return at night. Goes Fleance with you?'. Banquo's ghost appears to Macbeth at the banquet and he knows that Fleance has escaped death. In order to find out what is in store for him he again visits the witches. This time Macbeth takes part in the evil ritual; this shows how low he has sunk.

- The witches show him a head wearing armour and tell him to beware Macduff. Macduff has gone to join Malcolm in England. In order to solve this problem Macbeth later sends his men to murder Macduff's wife and children.

- The second apparition is a child covered in blood and it tells Macbeth that no one born of woman will hurt him. He immediately thinks he is invincible because we are all born of woman. The witches are tricking him again. He believes what he wants to believe. When he faces Macduff he realises that Macduff was taken early from his mother's womb, i.e. a Caesarian birth. At first Macbeth refuses to fight, but then changes his mind and Macduff kills him.

- The third vision is of a child holding a tree. Again Macbeth thinks that it is impossible that he will ever be beaten because the wood cannot move.

- He believes himself to be more invincible than ever and can do what he pleases. In fact Malcolm's troops cut branches from the wood and use them as camouflage as they move. It just looks as if the trees are moving. Again the witches have tricked Macbeth – as evil does. Finally they show him a line of kings – Banquo's children will succeed him, so his throne will never be safe.

- When he gets back to his castle he isolates himself, believing that he cannot be killed. Lady Macbeth kills herself but he shows no remorse. The English army succeeds and the prophecies come true.

National Curriculum Levels

The following are National Curriculum Writing criteria for levels 4 and 6. Judge work by how many of the features are included and how effectively. Imagine a line marked off in levels 4 to 7. Where does the answer fit on that line according to the criteria below?

Level 4	Level 6
The pupils' ideas are generally clear. There is some attempt to organise them into a suitable form. Pupils are beginning to choose words effectively. There is some use of grammatically correct sentences. Punctuation to mark sentences is mostly used accurately and pupils are beginning to use punctuation within the sentence. Spelling of simple and common longer words is generally accurate. Handwriting is mostly clear and legible.	The pupils' writing is interesting in parts, using suitable style for the task. The quality of the writing is enhanced by a varied vocabulary, a range of simple and complex sentences and appropriate paragraphing. A range of punctuation is usually used correctly to clarify meaning. Spelling is usually accurate. Handwriting is in a fluent and legible form.

The English Tests taken together are worth a total of 100 marks. Use the following table to find what overall level you might be working at.

Score	Criteria	NC Level
93–100	Exceptional answers	Level 7+
75–92	Well above average answers	Level 7
56–74	Above average answers	Level 6
40–55	Average or below average answers	Level 5
20–39	Well below average answers	Level 4 or below

Science

Science at Key Stage 3

You can specifically improve your marks in your Science Test by taking into account the following points:

The language used in the questions

1. The examiners will not put any useless information in a question. If something is written down then the examiner wants you to use it.
   - **Example:** *Space probes have shown that there are **mountains**, **dry river valleys** and **volcanoes** on Mars. Scientists believe Mars, like Earth, has all three types of rock: **igneous**, **metamorphic** and **sedimentary**. You will need to use all the terms.*

2. Use the mark scheme to tell you how many points you should include in your answers.

3. Read the question very carefully.
   - **Example** *Tick the correct box.* Only tick one box. If you tick more than one box, the question will be marked incorrect.

4. Don't be put off if you encounter unfamiliar material. You will know enough science to answer the question. In the example above you may not know much about Mars. However, the work you have done on rock formation on Earth will let you answer the question.

Key words found in the questions

1. **Choose** from a list of words. Make sure you use words from the list. Unless the paper states otherwise, you can use words more than once. Similarly you don't have to use them all.

2. **Describe...** You do **not** have to explain anything; you simply have to make a physical description of a diagram, graph etc.

3. **Explain...** You need to include a scientific explanation for your answer. Include some key scientific words in your answer.

4. **Predict...** There are two possible types of prediction:
   - Predicting what you think might happen in an investigation.
   - Extrapolating a graph (continuing a trend) to predict what might happen in the future.

5. Be aware of **negatives**.
   Example: *Give the name of another metal, **not** in the table...*

6. **Advantages and disadvantages.** To be on the safe side, make sure you state both things in your comparisons.

7. **Name... Which... What... Give...** These are simple command words which require a simple response. These are often found with numbers or words in bold type.

Sitting the practice test

This practice test is designed to help you get used to test conditions. When you take the tests in May you will be given an exact time (1 hour) and be expected to work in silence with no books or other person to help you. That is exactly how you should practise.

1. You need a pencil or pen and a watch or clock.

2. Ask someone to time the test so that you have exactly **60 minutes**.

3. If you cannot read a scientific word then someone can read it to you. That person should not tell you what it means.

Science at Key Stage 3

4. Do not start answering the questions until you have had a look at all of the test paper. This will give you a good idea of what is covered in the test and how many questions there are.

5. Read each question carefully and follow the instructions.

6. Do not spend too long over any one question. Answer it and move on.

7. If you can't answer a question, don't worry. Move on to the next one. You can always come back at the end.

8. Try to use all the time available. If you think you have finished, go back and check every question.

9. At the end of the time, check your answers with the mark scheme and work out your total.

10. Make a list of the questions you did not do too well on, but congratulate yourself on those you answered well.

11. Discuss the questions you found most difficult with a parent or a teacher. It is a good idea to check your notes to make sure that the topic won't cause problems again.

12. After a few weeks, try the questions again. You will improve your score if you have been working and revising and you will be well prepared for the real thing.

Refer to page **108** to find out what National Curriculum level you might be working at.

Science Test

1. The information in the table shows the recommended daily amounts of nutrients and energy for different people.

Person	Energy	Protein	Iron	Calcium
Farm worker	12 000 kJ	60 g	10 mg	650 mg
Office worker	10 000 kJ	58 g	10 mg	650 mg
15-year-old boy	11 000 kJ	54 g	11 mg	950 mg
15-year-old girl	8 000 kJ	44 g	15 mg	800 mg

(approximate values)

a) Give one reason why the office worker needs a lower-energy diet than the farm worker.

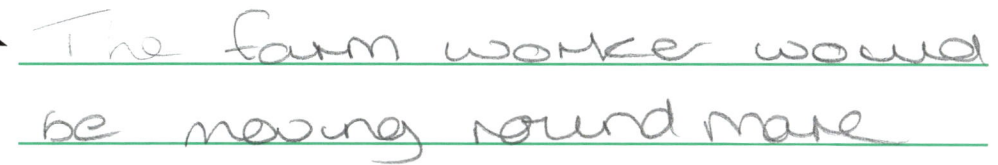

The farm worker would be moving round more

b) Iron is needed to make red blood cells. Explain why 15-year-old girls need more iron than 15-year-old boys.

When girls have periods they lose blood so they need more blood cells.

c) Give one reason why 15-year-old boys and girls need more calcium than adults.

There bones are still growing

TOTAL 3

Science Test

d i Which of the following foods would be the best source of calcium for the 15-year-olds?
Tick one box.

celery ☐   margarine ☐

milk ☑   chicken ☐

ii Which of the foods would be the best source of protein?
Tick one box.

celery ☐   margarine ☐

milk ☐   chicken ☑

iii Which of the foods would be the best source of fibre?
Tick one box.

celery ☑   margarine ☐

milk ☐   chicken ☐

TOTAL 3

Science Test

2 The diagram shows an important organ system in females.

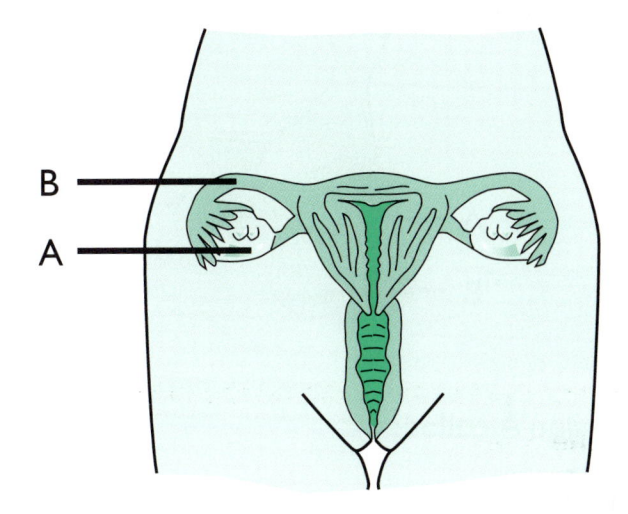

a What is the name of this organ system?

reprodutive system

b Eggs are produced in organ A. What is the name of organ A?

ovary

c The eggs travel down tube B. What is the name of tube B?

oviduct

Science Test

The diagram below shows the equivalent organ system in males.

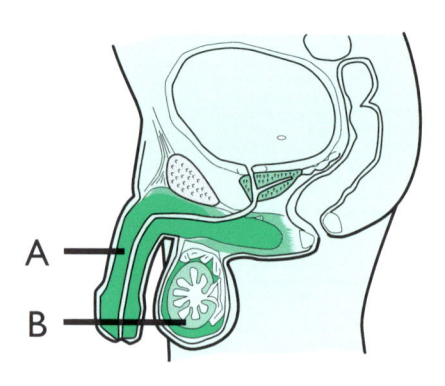

d What is organ A called?

Penis

1

e Sperm cells are made in organ B. What is organ B called?

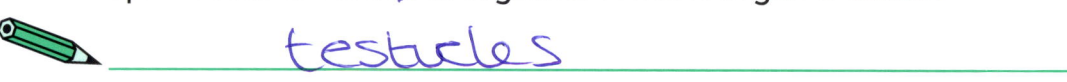

testicles

1

f Use the words below to complete the description.

| placenta | fertilised | embryo | divides | uterus | sperm |

6

When ___*sperm*___ cells meet an egg cell one of them may enter.

The egg cell is ___*fertilised*___. The egg cell then travels to the

___*uterus*___ where it becomes embedded in the thick wall. The

egg cell ___*divides*___ and develops into an ___*embryo*___. This

is given food from the mother via the ___*placenta*___.

TOTAL **8**

84

3a The diagram below shows human lungs.

i Write the names of A, B and C.

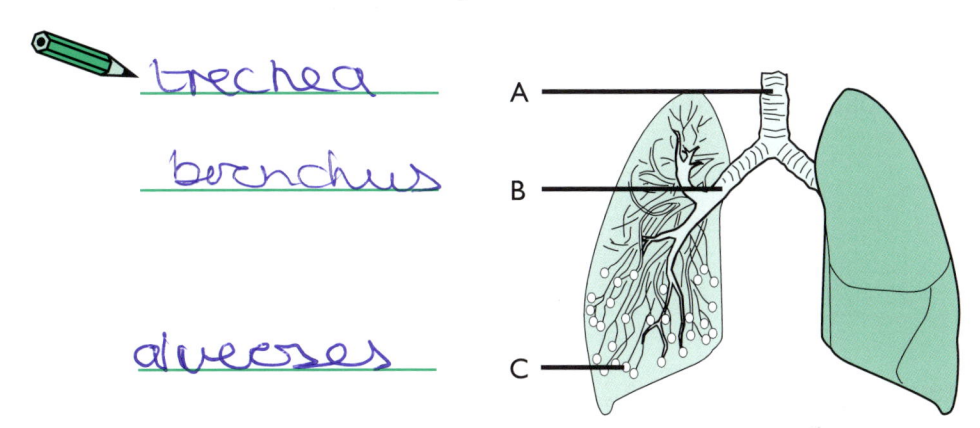

A — *trechea*
B — *bronchus*
C — *alveeses*

ii In each lung there are many branches. Each branch ends at the part labelled C.
Explain how this arrangement helps humans to breathe more effectively.

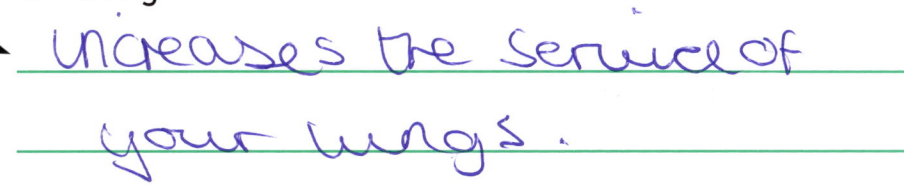

increases the service of your lungs.

iii Part A has rings of material called cartilage. Suggest **one** reason why these rings of cartilage are present.

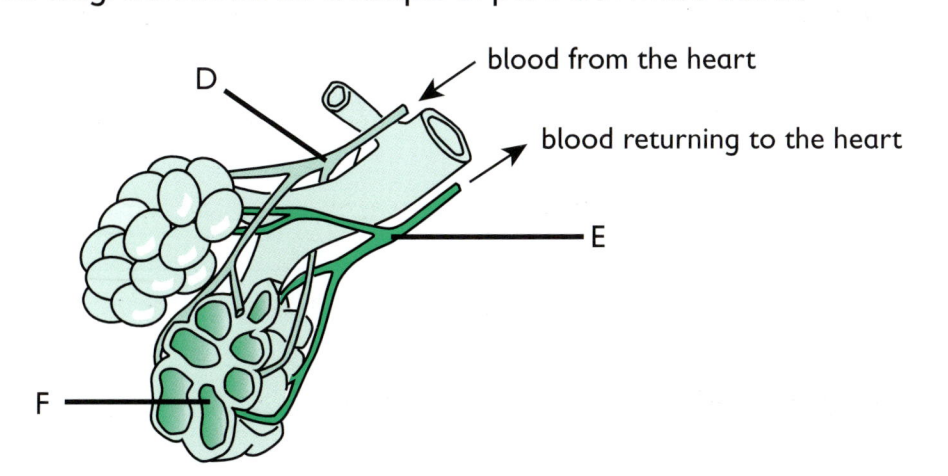

b The diagram shows an example of part C in more detail.

blood from the heart
blood returning to the heart
D
E
F

3

1

1

TOTAL
5

85

Science Test

i Give one reason why part F has such a rich blood supply.

_____

ii Describe **two** differences between the blood flowing in capillary D and the blood flowing in capillary E.

1. _____

2. _____

c Stewart was being tested for asthma. He was asked to breathe into a machine to test how much air he could breathe into and out of his lungs.

i How much air did Stewart manage to breathe out into the machine?

_____

Air contains nitrogen, oxygen, carbon dioxide, noble gases and water vapour.

ii Give **two** differences between the composition of the air Stewart breathed in and the air he breathed out into the machine.

1. _____

2. _____

86

4 The diagram below shows the particles in a solid, a liquid and a gas. Each arrow represents a change of state.

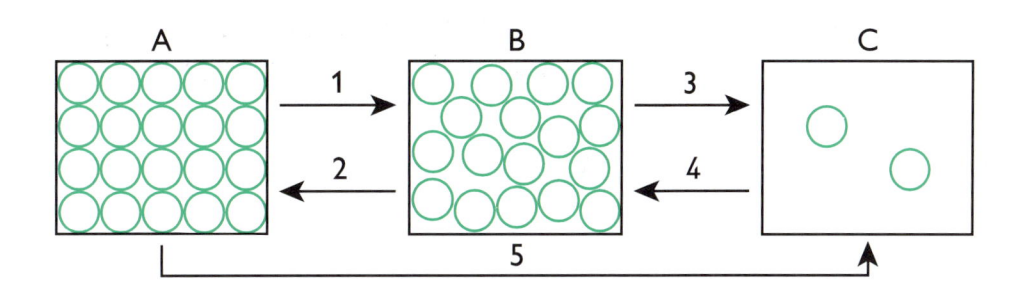

```
    A           B           C
            1→          3→
            ←2          ←4
            ←——————5——————
```

a Which diagram represents a solid?

a

Explain your answer.

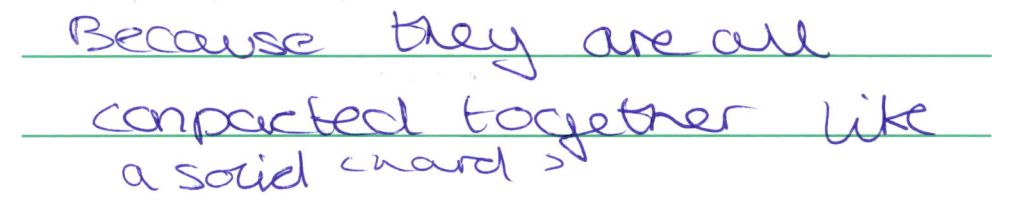

Because they are all compacted together like a solid chard>

b Which diagram represents a gas?

C

Explain your answer.

Because they are apart

Science Test

c Look at the diagram on page 87. Choose from the list of words to complete the sentences below.

condensation	sublimation	freezing
evaporation	boiling	melting

Change of state 1 is called _____

Change of state 2 is called _____

Change of state 3 is called _____

Change of state 4 is called _____

Change of state 5 is called _____

d Which change of state is being used during the following processes?

Separating water from salt by heating the water.

_____

Drying clothes on a washing line.

_____

Making ice cubes from water.

_____

TOTAL 8

88

Science Test

5 The diagram below shows an investigation to examine rusting.

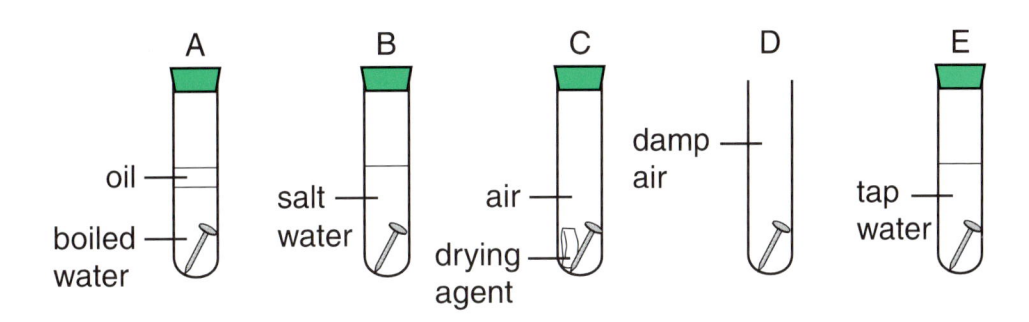

A: oil, boiled water
B: salt water
C: air, drying agent
D: damp air
E: tap water

The table shows how each test tube was set up.

Tube	Treatment
A	A clean nail was covered with boiled water (to remove dissolved air) then covered with a layer of oil.
B	A clean nail was added to salty water.
C	A clean nail was added to a tube with air in. A drying agent was added to dry the air.
D	A clean nail was added to a tube of air, which was left open.
E	A clean nail was added to tap water.

All the tubes were then left for 5 days.

a Which nail would you expect to be the most rusty after 5 days?

The nail in tube ___B___

Explain your answer.

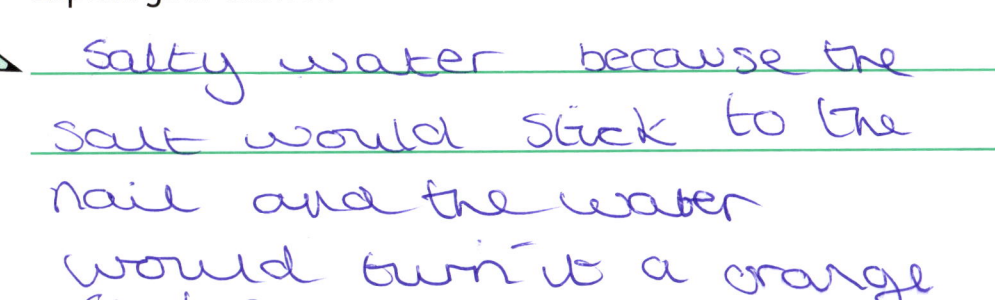

Salty water because the salt would stick to the nail and the water would turn it a orange color

2

TOTAL

2

Science Test

b Below is a list of substances that occur naturally. Complete the table by putting **two** ticks in each row.

Substance	element	compound	atom	molecule
O_2				
N_2				
CO_2				
Ne				
H_2O				
$CaCO_3$				

TOTAL 6

7a A tow truck is trying to pull a car along a level road. The car's brakes are on and the car does not move.

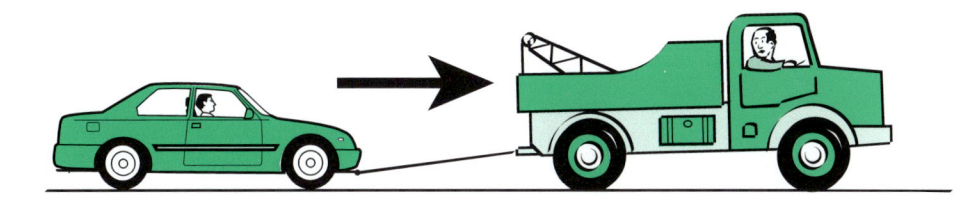

i Draw **one** arrow on the diagram to show the direction of the force which prevents the car from moving.

ii Is the force of the pull of the tow truck **less than**, **equal to** or **more than** the force which prevents the car from moving?

_____

b When the car's brakes are off, the tow truck pulls the car forwards. Another force (force X) works to slow the car down.

i What is the name of force X?

_____

ii In what direction does this force act?

_____

Science Test

iii The pull of the tow truck is 4000 N. As the car's speed increases, how large is force X?

Tick the correct box.

More than 4000 N ☐   4000 N ☐

Between 0 and 4000 N ☐   zero ☐

iv After a few minutes, the car travels at a steady speed. The tow truck is still pulling with a force of 4000 N.

How large is force X now?

_____

TOTAL

8 Fatima is trying to remove a wheel from her car. She is trying to release the wheel nuts with a spanner. The diagram shows the size of the force she is exerting and where the force acts on the spanner.

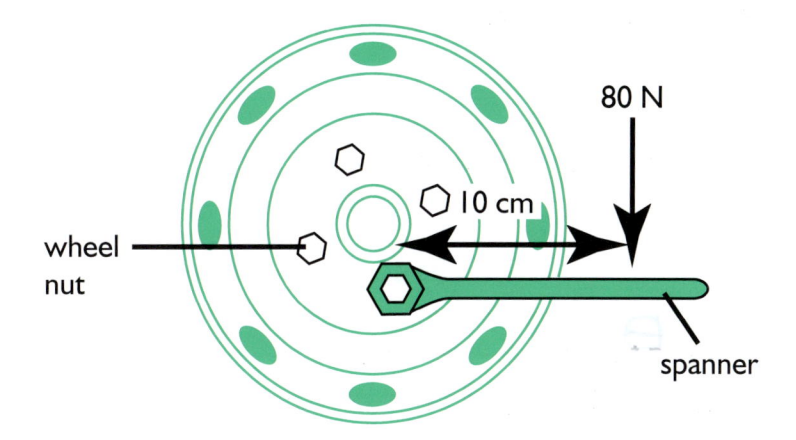

a The spanner applies a turning effect (moment) to a wheel nut. Calculate the size of the moment. Give the units.

b The wheel nut will not move. Give **two** ways in which Fatima could increase the moment she applies to the spanner.

1. _____

2. _____

Science Test

9 Look at the circuit diagrams below:

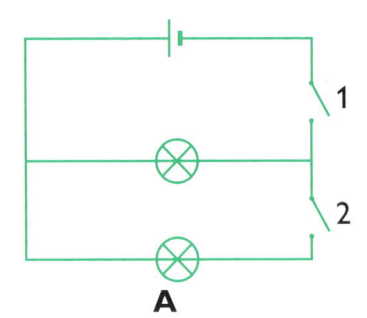

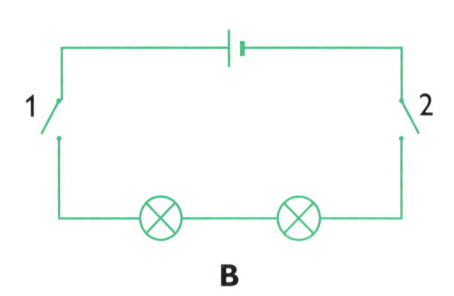

A   B

a Which circuit has the bulbs connected in series?

B

b The switches in the circuits are closed. If the voltage of the cells in A and B are the same:

   i In which circuit will the bulbs be brightest?

   A

   ii If one of the bulbs in circuit B was blown, what would happen to the other?

   the circuit would not work.

   iii Explain what you would see in circuit A if switch 1 was closed and switch 2 was open.

   only one bulb would light.

The same circuits were set up again but this time ammeters were added and the switches removed. Ammeters are devices for measuring current. The units used are called amperes or amps (A).

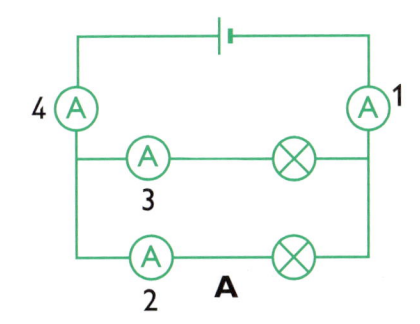

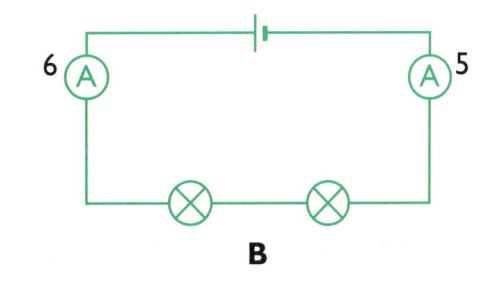

A

B

c i Complete the table by writing in the correct number of amps.

All bulbs are identical.

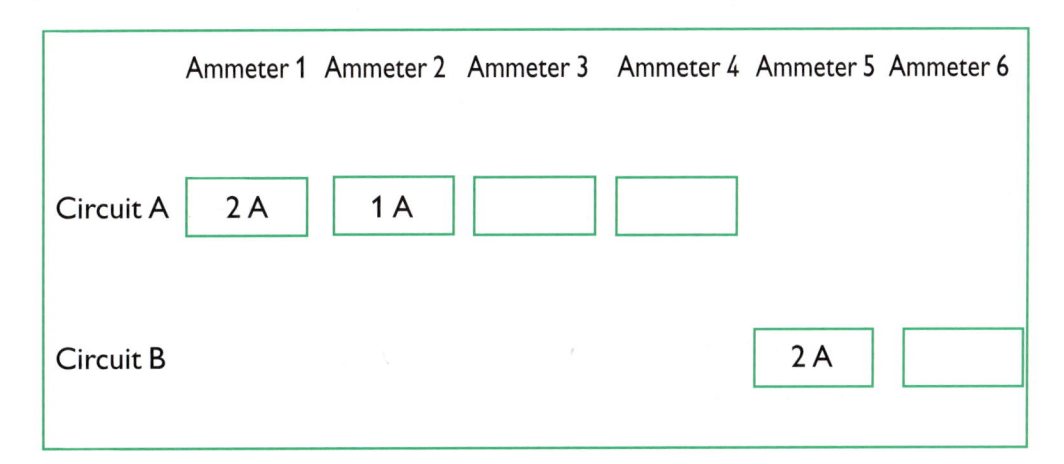

	Ammeter 1	Ammeter 2	Ammeter 3	Ammeter 4	Ammeter 5	Ammeter 6
Circuit A	2 A	1 A				
Circuit B					2 A	

ii Explain your reasons for all three answers.

_____

_____

_____

TOTAL

5

97

Science Test

10 The diagram shows part of a food web.

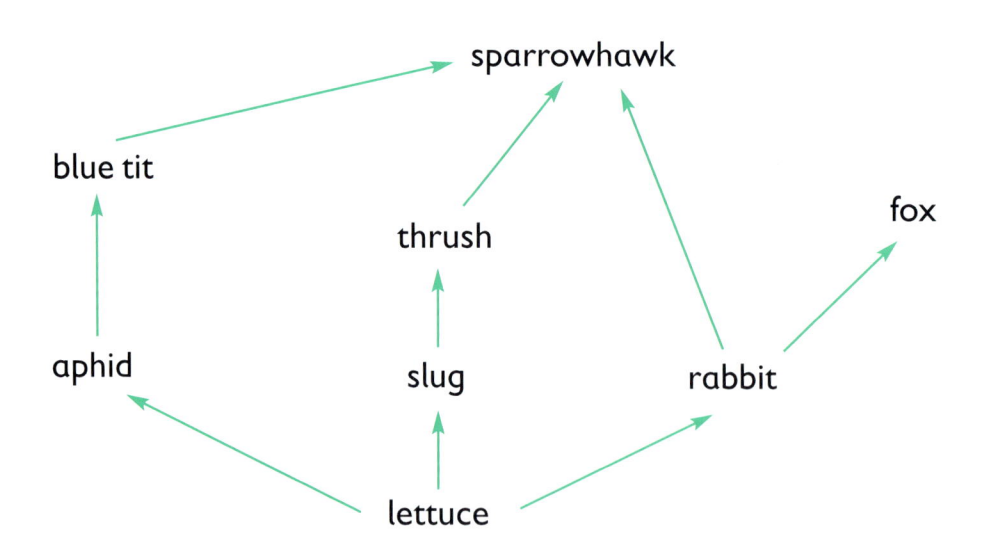

[Food web diagram showing: lettuce → aphid, slug, rabbit; aphid → blue tit; slug → thrush; blue tit → sparrowhawk; thrush → sparrowhawk; rabbit → sparrowhawk; rabbit → fox]

Use **only** the information in the diagram above to answer the following questions.

a Name **one** carnivore and **one** herbivore.

carnivore ___Sparrow hawk___

herbivore ___slug___

b A predator is an animal that catches smaller animals to eat. Give the name of one predator and the name of one of its prey.

predator ___fox___

prey ___rabbit___

TOTAL: 4

c If the number of rabbits in a particular habitat decreases, this affects the numbers of other animals living there. Use the food web to explain:

i Why the number of slugs might increase.

because all the rabbits would of ait the lettuces.

ii Why the number of foxes might decrease.

because there is enough food for everyone.

iii Why the number of thrushes might increase.

because the thrush don't have any thing to eat = slugs.

iv Why the number of thrushes might decrease.

Sparrow might catch all the thrush when theres fewer rabbits.

d The lettuce in the food web was sprayed with an insecticide. Explain why small amounts of the insecticide were found in the tissues of sparrowhawks.

because the sparrow ait the thrush, which ait the slug then the slug ait lettuce which was infected.

Science Test

11 The table below shows the pH of five common substances.

Substance	pH
Vinegar	3
Fruit juice	4
Pure water	7
Soap	8
Detergent	11

a Which two substances are acidic?

1. vinigar
2. Ditergent

b Which two substances are alkaline?

1. fruit juice
2. soap

swap

c Which substance is neutral?

pure water

TOTAL 5

d Wasp stings are alkaline.
Which substance from the table could you rub on a wasp sting to stop it hurting?

Vinigar, fruit juice

Explain your answer.

Because the vingar will nutralise the sting

e Sometimes soil is too acidic to allow certain crops to grow.
A farmer may decide to add lime to the soil to make the soil less acidic.

i Is lime an acid or an alkali?

✗ acid / alkali ✓

ii Name the process of adding a substance to an acid to make the pH 7.

nutralise

TOTAL 4

101

Science Test

12

a can of cold cola in a fridge 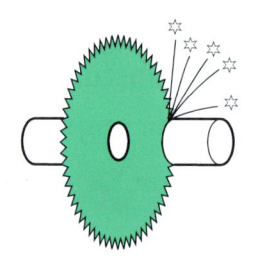   white-hot sparks from a cutter

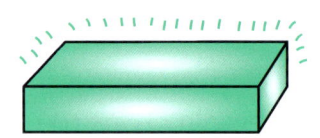

a slab of iron glowing red-hot 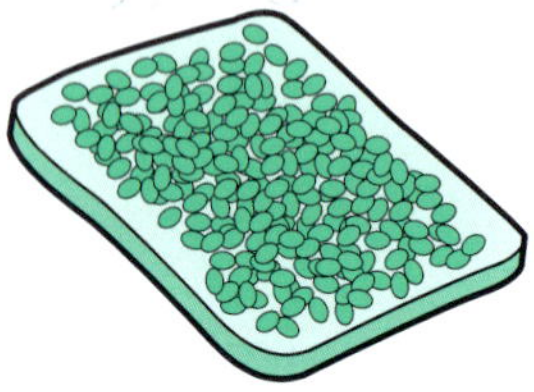   freshly cooked beans on toast

a Each of the four objects shown above started at room temperature. Now they are all at different temperatures.

i Which object has lost thermal energy?

Cola

ii Which object has had the largest gain in thermal energy?

Slap of iron

iii Which object is at the highest temperature?

White hot sparks.

TOTAL 3

102

b Samantha puts a hot spoon into a glass of water. She leaves it for ten minutes.

i What will happen to the temperature of the water during the ten minutes?

it will rise

Explain your answer.

ii What will happen to the temperature of the spoon during the ten minutes?

it will fall

Explain your answer.

Science Test

c Look at the table below. Column 1 shows the thermal energy stored in the spoon and the water before the experiment. Column 2 shows the thermal energy in the spoon and the water after ten minutes.

	1 before	2 after ten minutes
Spoon	9800 J	6800 J
Water	4400 J	6800 J

i Calculate how many joules of energy the spoon loses during the ten minutes.

ii Calculate how many joules of energy have been gained by the water during the ten minutes.

iii Calculate the difference between the loss of energy from the spoon and the gain in energy by the water.

iv What has happened to the energy in part iii?

Science

Answers

Question number	Answer	Mark
1a	An office worker will not be moving around as much and so will need less energy.	1
1b	Most 15-year-old girls have started menstruation and so will lose blood every month.	1
1c	15-year-old boys and girls are still growing and need calcium for bones.	1
1d	i. milk ii. chicken iii. celery	1 1 1
2a	reproductive system	1
2b	ovary	1
2c	oviduct *or* fallopian tube	1
2d	penis	1
2e	testicle	1
2f	sperm, fertilised, uterus, divides, embryo, placenta	6

3a	i. A = trachea
	   B = bronchus
	   C = alveolus
	ii. The alveoli increase the surface area of the lungs.
	iii. To strengthen the trachea and stop it from collapsing.
		3
		
		1
		1

3b	i. To let gases into and out of the blood. ii. 1. Blood in capillary D has more carbon dioxide. 2. Blood in capillary E has more oxygen.	1 2
3c	i. 4000 cm^3 ii. 1. The air he breathed in was richer in oxygen than the air he breathed out. 2. The air he breathed out was richer in carbon dioxide than the air he breathed in.	1 2
4a	A The particles are closely packed together in a regular structure.	1 1
4b	C The particles are very far apart.	1 1
4c	1 = melting, 2 = freezing, 3 = evaporation or boiling, 4 = condensation, 5 = sublimation	5

Science Answers

Question number	Answer	Mark
4d	evaporation or boiling evaporation freezing	3
5a	B Salt makes things rust faster.	2
5b	A *or* C Rusting needs oxygen and water. Tube A has little oxygen in it. Tube C has little moisture	2
5c	Temperature must be kept constant. Identical nails must be used.	2
5d	i. Any two from painting/oiling/coating with a more reactive metal such as zinc. ii. oxidation	2 1
6a	malachite *or* marble salt gold diamond (carbon) bauxite	5
6b	element and molecule element and molecule compound and molecule element and atom compound and molecule compound and molecule	6
7a	i. There should be an arrow pointing left (opposite to the arrow already on the diagram). ii. equal	1 1
7b	i. friction ii. to the left iii. between 0 and 4000 N iv. 4000 N	1 1 1 1
8a	80 N × 10 cm = 800 Ncm	2
8b	1. Increase the force she applies. 2. Apply the force further away from the fulcrum (pivot).	2
9a	B	1
9b	i. A ii. The other bulb would go out. iii. Only one bulb would light – the one nearest to the cell.	1 1 1

Science Answers

Question number	Answer	Mark

9c	i. Circuit A Ammeter 3 = 1 A
	                   Ammeter 4 = 2 A
	     Circuit B Ammeter 6 = 2 A
	 ii. The parallel circuit allows the two identical bulbs to share the current and so each branch will have 1 A. The current in the series circuit is the same throughout.
		3
		
		 2

10a	sparrowhawk, fox, blue tit or thrush slug, aphid or rabbit	2
10b	predator = sparrowhawk prey = blue tit/thrush/rabbit or predator = fox prey = rabbit or predator = thrush prey = slug	2
10c	i. There will less competition for lettuce. ii. There will not be enough food to support the population. iii. More slugs could result in an increased population of thrushes. iv. Sparrowhawks might catch more thrushes as there are fewer rabbits.	1 1 1 1
10d	The insecticide was passed from lettuce to slugs then from slugs to thrushes and finally to sparrowhawks as the various living things were eaten.	1
11a	1. vinegar 2. fruit juice	2
11b	1. soap 2. detergent	2
11c	pure water	1
11d	vinegar or fruit juice The acidic substance will neutralise the alkaline sting.	2
11e	i. alkali ii. neutralisation	1 1
12a	i. can of cola ii. slab of red-hot iron iii. white-hot sparks from a cutter	1 1 1

12b	i. It will rise.
	     Thermal energy from the spoon will warm up the water.
	 ii. It will fall.
	      Thermal energy is lost to the cooler water.
		1
		 1
		 1
		 1

12c	i. 3000 J ii. 2400 J iii. 600 J iv. It has been given out to the environment as heat.	1 1 1 1

National Curriculum Levels

Maximum marks: 108

Mark	0–40	41–56	57–72	73–91	92–107
Level	Below Level 4	Level 4	Level 5	Level 6	Level 7

If you need more practice in any Science topics, you should use the WHSmith Key Stage 3 Science Revision Guide.